P9-ASF-442

Rome and Russia

A TRAGEDY OF ERRORS

"If there is not a Christian revival in the world, a rebirth not only among the elite but also among the great masses of the people, atheistic Communism will conquer over the whole earth."

NICHOLAS BERDYAEV

Rome and Russia

A TRAGEDY OF ERRORS

BY SISTER MARY JUST
OF MARYKNOLL

THE NEWMAN PRESS · 1954 · WESTMINSTER, MARYLAND

Nihil obstat: Edward A. Cerny, S.S.
Censor Librorum

Imprimatur: Francis P. Keough, D.D.
Archbishop of Baltimore

August 3, 1954

The *nihil obstat* and *imprimatur* are official declarations that a book or pamphlet is free of doctrinal and moral error. No implication is contained therein that those who have granted the *nihil obstat* and *imprimatur* agree with the opinions expressed.

Library of Congress Catalog Card Number: 54-12078

Printed in the United States of America

To my brother, E. V. DAVID

Acknowledgments

AMONG *the chief sources consulted for this study are the authoritative five volumes of* La Russie et le Saint-Siège, *by the Russian Jesuit, Father Paul Pierling; and the two-volume continuation of Father Pierling's work,* Le Saint-Siège et la Russie, *by his Jesuit pupil, Father Adrien Boudou.* Russia's Attitude Towards Union With Rome *(9th–16th centuries), by Monsignor Joseph B. Koncius (Koncevicius), is a valuable guide for the years preceding the period covered in Father Pierling's volumes. The works of Helen Iswolsky and of the late George P. Fedotov present vividly revealing aspects of the religious soul of Russia. In addition to the works on Russia and Rome mentioned above, numerous other sources of information are listed in the bibliography.*

Introduction

SINCE the middle of the fifteenth century, when Czar Basil II rejected union with the Holy See, no other country of comparable size and importance has so consistently and completely baffled the Catholic apostolate as Russia. The reasons for this attitude are inextricably intertwined with the nation's singular history.

When the royal apostle, Prince Vladimir of Kiev, led his people to Christianity toward the close of the tenth century, the Eastern Church was not in actual schism from Rome. But from the first, Russian rulers were affected by the Caesaropapism of Constantinople and were consequently inclined to interfere in the spiritual jurisdiction of the Church.

Because Kievan Russia had many ties with Western Europe, the relations between Russia and the Holy See were preserved intact for about a century and a half after the Greek Schism of 1054. But the majority of the early prelates in Russia were Greeks, and they infected their flocks with hatred of Latin Christianity. As the Kievan realm broke up under the attacks of Asiatic nomads, Russia was assailed by Catholic neighbors on the west. Hostility to Catholicism increased, because it was the religion of these Western enemies. In the early years of the thirteenth century, the ties between Russia and the Holy See were definitely sundered.

In the thirteenth century a new Russia, shut off from the outside world and under the Tartar yoke, grew up in the forests far north of Kiev. Gradually the cunning princes of Moscow rose to supremacy, and the new Russia eventually bore the name of Muscovy. Hostility to the Latin Church increased steadily among the isolated, ignorant, and embattled Muscovites. As the power of the Muscovite rulers waxed, they became increasingly desirous of governing the Russian Church without the "interference" of any Latin Pontiff. The Muscovites were resolved to retake the Russian territories conquered by the Catholic Poles; and, on their part, the Poles impeded papal attempts to establish diplomatic relations with "barbaric" Russia.

Ivan III (1462–1505) cast off the Tartar yoke. When he ascended the throne, Constantinople, "the second Rome," had fallen to the Turks. Ivan married the niece of the last Byzantine Emperor, and thought himself the successor of the Greek rulers as the head of the Eastern Church. Now Moscow, "the third Rome," alone preserved "the pure deposit of faith." To Russia had been given the spiritual leadership of the world! These messianic ideas penetrated the masses and became part of popular Russian tradition.

Succeeding Russian Czars had recourse to the diplomatic services of Rome, when it was to their own interest; otherwise, almost all of them manifested an ingrained hostility to the Holy See. During the "Time of Troubles" which followed the reign of Ivan the Terrible (1533–1584), Poland invaded Russia and Catholics installed themselves in the very Kremlin. Poles and Catholicism were thereafter inextricably associated in the patriotic hatred of the Russian people.

A further cause of Russian enmity to Rome was the foundation of the Ruthenian Uniate Church in Poland, in 1596. The Ruthenians were of Russian ancestry and had abandoned Orthodoxy, "the one pure faith." From then on the majority of the Czars seized every opportunity of persecuting Russian Uniates.

Under Catherine the Great (1762–1796) the successive partitions of Poland subjected millions of Catholics, Latin and Uniate, to Russian rule. It became the Czarist policy, in regard to the Latin Catholics in the Empire, to found a "National Catholic Church," having vastly weakened ties with the Holy See. This policy, in a more brazen and brutal form, has been continued by the Soviet rulers.

From the time of their seizure of power in November, 1917, the Bolsheviks considered the Catholic Church as the chief adversary. By 1939, Soviet persecution of Catholicism in Russia proper had brought about its complete disorganization. During and after World War II, Stalin revived in a sovietized form the tradition of a Muscovite "third Rome," by using the National Russian Church as a propaganda weapon against the Vatican. The postwar expansion of Russia has subjected more than sixty million Catholics of Eastern Europe to Communist persecution, while the advance of Communist control in Asia endangers the Catholic missions of that continent.

The otherwise dispiriting study of the Holy See's centuries-long, frustrated efforts to achieve reunion with Russia leads to an amazingly consoling conclusion. We see that the rejection of the union was never national, but solely the work of successive despotic rulers who always prevented free access of Catholic apostles to the Russian masses. Until now, the oppressed millions of Russia have glimpsed Catholicism only under the caricatured likeness of hated Western foes. Today, the most stirring hope of the Catholic apostolate is that of the time when it would at last be possible to reveal the true image of the worldwide Church to a people invincibly drawn to universalism.

Contents

Rome and Russia
A TRAGEDY OF ERRORS

CHAPTER ONE

Kievan Glory and Decline

IN THE early centuries of the Christian era, the vast, flat lands of the region later to be known as European Russia rolled on in monotonous beauty to far horizons. These immense expanses seemed strangely empty of human habitation, but hidden in the great forests south of the frozen marshes and the crawling scrub of the Arctic regions were primitive dwellings of the Finns. Over the southern steppes nomads roamed on wiry steeds, warring with one another and plundering the vanquished. In the southwestern corner of the vast region, a blond and seemingly unimportant people, the Eastern Slavs, dwelt along the waterways as peaceful cultivators. They were beginning to expand northward and eastward from the slopes and spurs of the Carpathian Mountains.

In the immense, flat lands inhabited by the Finns, the nomads, and the Eastern Slavs there was the foundation for a mighty nation. Neither Finns nor nomads were to be the people of destiny, but the earliest folk songs of the blond Eastern Slavs are alive with a world-sense. During the decades that followed the crucifixion of Christ the civilized world had no conception of the destiny of the Eastern Slavs; in fact, it knew practically nothing about them.

During the seventh century before Christ numerous Greek colonies had been founded on the northern shore of the Black Sea, and they continued to serve as intermediaries of the commerce between the barbaric peoples of what is now Russia and the civilized towns of Greece. In the fifth century before Christ the Greek historian, Herodotus, wrote about the cruel Scythians who roamed the steppes north of the Greek commercial colonies. Though the Scythians were later vanquished by other Indo-European nomads, the ancient world continued to call the region north of the Black Sea, Scythia.

According to the Legends

Eusebius, Bishop of Caesarea (c. 260–340), stated in his *Church History* that the Apostle Saint Andrew evangelized the Scythians. The early Christian traditions of Russia relate that the Apostle of Scythia set sail up the magnificent Dnieper River, on his way to visit in Rome his brother, Saint Peter. Some five hundred miles from the mouth of the Dnieper, Saint Andrew saw from the river the heights of Kiev, then bare and solitary.

The Apostle disembarked and planted a cross on this eminence. Then he said to his companions, "See you those hills? On those heights shall hereafter shine forth the Grace of God. There shall be a great city upon this spot, and God shall cause many churches to rise within it." [1]

The legendary accounts of the life of Pope Saint Clement describe how he evangelized the peoples of southern Russia and assert that he was martyred in the Crimea about 97 A.D. In the ninth century Saints Cyril and Methodius, when preaching the faith to the Khazars in the Crimea, discovered what they believed to be the relics of Pope Saint Clement.[2] The brother apostles presented their treasure to Pope Adrian

II. Russian history contains a number of references to representatives of the Holy See who brought gifts of holy relics to Saint Vladimir at Kiev. It is thought that these presents were relics of Pope Saint Clement.

A Peace-loving People

In spite of the various poetic legends of the early Russian Church, it is certain that the great majority of the Eastern Slavs remained pagan until the tenth century. They continued their expansion northward and eastward from the Carpathians, hampered by successive westward waves of onrushing nomads. They served as a bulwark of Europe against Asia and suffered some of the hardest blows struck by nomadic invaders from the East. Yet the Eastern Slavs were by nature a peace-loving people, so much so that after their conversion to Christianity they transformed Saint George, patron of warriors, into a village shepherd and a farmer.

Farming was the principal occupation of the primitive Russians. They also hunted, fished, and engaged in the culture of bees. Severe climate and hard living conditions gave tough strength to their physique and character. They were a cheerful, warmhearted, expansive, and hospitable people, fond of song, dancing, music, and glowing colors. "The broad Russian nature" is an ancient Russian phrase. The pagan Eastern Slavs were a religious people, who with poetic imagination deified the phenomena of nature. They had a dim conception of a Supreme Being who in the course of time came to be worshiped under the name of Perun, the thunder-maker.

Russia is a land of splendid waterways. The Eastern Slavs spread far out into the basin of the Don. In the seventh century, they ascended the Dnieper and founded the city of Kiev. To the north, on the Volkhov River, was founded at an early, unknown date the trading center of Novgorod, linked to Kiev by the Volkhov, Lovat, Dvina, Pripet, Desna, and Dnieper

Rivers. This great water road was the first Russia, which developed as a commercial state, trading with Constantinople, Asia Minor, and Mesopotamia.

Viking Rulers in Russia

In addition to the Eastern Slavs, another people, the Viking warrior-traders of Scandinavia, contributed to the growth of the Russian water road. Increasing numbers of enterprising Swedish companies, the so-called Varangians, journeyed in armed bands to Constantinople along this river-trade artery. Many Varangians began to remain in the Russian commercial towns, especially in Novgorod and in Kiev.

The Russian Chronicle ascribed to Nestor, a monk of the famous Kievan Monastery of the Caves, relates how the people of Novgorod invited the Viking leader, Rurik, to become their prince (862). The savage Asiatic Pechenegs had occupied both banks of the lower Dnieper, and the commercial artery of the Eastern Slavs was in grave peril. "Our land is great and fruitful, but there is no order in it," the Novgorodians told Rurik. "Come and reign over us!" [3]

On Rurik's death, his kinsman, Oleg, became prince of Novgorod. In 882, Oleg sailed down to Kiev and established himself there also as ruler. This event may be regarded as the foundation of the Russian State. The name Rus had been used to designate the Swedish companies and their chiefs. Now the name Russia was given to the region of Kiev, and later to all the lands united under the scepter of the Prince of Kiev.

A few of the Varangians in the Russian towns may have been Christians. In any case, the Eastern Slavs were coming into contact with Christianity in Constantinople. A Byzantine chronicle relates that Russian pirates from Kiev attacked Constantinople in the summer of the year 860. The Russians were repulsed with disastrous losses. A considerable number of the Kievan adventurers, impressed by the mighty protection the Christian God had given to the Greeks, accepted Christianity soon afterwards. The Patriarch of Constantinople thereupon sent missioners to Kiev.

Igor, the successor of Oleg, led an expedition to Constantinople in the year 945. In the treaty concluded by Igor with the Greeks there is express mention of the fact that many of the Russian ruler's warriors were Christians. We learn from the Chronicles that these Christians had their own place of worship in Kiev, the wooden Church of St. Ilya, or Elias.

Saint Olga's Grandson

Igor's widow, Olga, who ruled with energy during the minority of her son, embraced the Christian religion. Princess Olga was baptized about the year 958, probably at Kiev. But the mass of the Kievan warriors kept Christianity at a distance. Olga was unable to make a Christian of her own son, Svyatoslav. "My warrior companions would laugh at me!," objected this typical Viking prince.[4]

Saint Olga asked Emperor Otto I of Germany to send missioners to Russia. Bishop Adalbert, later Archbishop of Magdeburg, was sent to Kiev in 961. His mission was not successful, and this may well have been because Olga was then no longer regent. In 972 the warrior-ruler, Svyatoslav, was killed by the Pechenegs, who made a drinking cup of his skull. During the brief reign of Svyatoslav's son, Yaropolk, Pope Benedict VII sent envoys to Russia in 979. The chroniclers record this visit, but they do not shed any light on its purpose or outcome.

The mild Yaropolk was murdered in 980, and was succeeded by Vladimir, a natural son of Svyatoslav and a fierce pagan who offered human sacrifices to Perun. The native poets called this tall, ruddy-haired young ruler Red Sun. On one occasion the pagan grandson of Saint Olga ordered Theodore, a Russian Christian, to surrender his son John as a sacrificial victim to Perun. Theodore refused, whereupon both father and son suffered death at the hands of the infuriated populace. They were the first Christian martyrs in Russia.

From the beginning of his reign Vladimir's great aim was to consolidate the Russian State. In this he was ably assisted by a group of armed companions, composed partly of boyars, or large landed proprietors, and partly of soldiers of fortune. This earliest Russian aristocracy enjoyed a large measure of independence. Peoples of Europe and of Asia became aware that a vigorous young nation was arising on the Russian plains, and missioners of various faiths arrived in Kiev, seeking to convert its pagan Grand Prince.

According to the traditional account of Vladimir's conversion, the Grand Prince examined carefully the claims of the various missioners. Attracted by the splendid Eastern Liturgy, he finally decided in favor of the Byzantine form of Christianity practiced in Constantinople. It seemed a good choice at a time when tenth-century Western Europe was plunged in the semibarbarism of the Dark Ages. The Clovis of the Russians could not then foresee that his people would eventually be engulfed in the tragedy of the Greek Schism, and would thereby be cut off from the main stream of European culture. Nor could he know that his decision was destined to become an age-long source of bitter enmity between Russia and neighboring Slavs who had made a different choice.[5]

Kiev Becomes a Christian Center

At the time of Prince Vladimir's baptism, in the year 988, he married Princess Anne, the daughter of the Greek Emperor, Basil II. He destroyed the pagan idols in Kiev and ordered all his subjects to repair to the Dnieper River. As the Russians were baptized in the broad stream, the ruler was happy that he and his people had found the true religion. Vladimir prayed, saying: "God, it is Thou Who hast created heaven and earth! Guard these, Thy new people, and allow them, O Lord, to discover the true God, such as the Christians know." [6]

Under the sway of the converted sovereign, schools and churches were built in the land. The early bishops came from Constantinople, but the Grand Prince was careful to educate the sons of his own aristocracy in order that there might be in time Russian clergy. He made Kiev a center of Christian influence, whence missioners journeyed into the interior of Russia, everywhere baptizing and instructing the people. But, needless to say, it required thereafter many centuries of apostolic endeavor to bring even the major portion of the vast land of Russia under Christian influence.

At the time of the conversion of Russia, Greek religious forms had already become static. In spite of this, the Russian offspring of the Church of Byzantium had a vital spirit. One of the chief reasons for the dynamism of the Russian Church was that it welcomed with joy the Byzantine liturgy in its Slavonic rendering. Russia received from Greece an organized and impressive hierarchy, in whose wake came artists who built magnificent churches adorned with rich icons. The artistic temperament of the Eastern Slavs was awakened and subjugated for good. Though it is true that the Greek prelates in Russia taught the average members of the native clergy only the rudiments of theology, recent research confirms the existence in Kievan society of an intellectual elite, both ecclesiastical and lay.

In young Russia, the temporal ruler spread the faith and the clergy carried out his orders. The Russian Church borrowed from Constantinople a form of State-Church relationship which gave the actual supremacy to the State. Nevertheless, during the Kievan period of Russian history the bishops took an active part in the civic life of their flock, and they often had greater influence than the princes.

The mainspring of Christian inspiration in early Russia was

the parish church, where the laity sang or read the major portion of the offices in the easily understood Slavonic. The moving words of the prayers and hymns sank into the hearts of the people, while their eyes beheld the spiritual beauty of the religious paintings which covered the walls and ceilings of church buildings.

Monasteries were founded in Russia soon after the nation's conversion. The Kievan monks were ready to assist lay people not only in their spiritual difficulties but also in their material concerns. These monks of young Russia believed that the whole of man's life must be illuminated by the splendor of the Holy Spirit. The lives of the monks of Kiev's Monastery of the Caves were written down and later collected in the famous *Paterikon,* long the favorite reading of the Russian masses.[7]

Ties With the West

Vladimir had close ties with Latin Christianity. His son Svyatopolk married the daughter of Boleslaw the Mighty of Poland. His sister-in-law became the wife of Emperor Otto II of Germany. The Grand Prince of Kiev cordially welcomed delegates from the Holy See in 988, in 994, and again in 1002. The Russian annals relate that the people of Kiev also greeted the papal envoys with joy.[8]

Prince Vladimir was invariably kind to missioners from the West, and one of the most hauntingly beautiful of the stories of ancient Russia describes his friendship with Saint Bruno of Querfurt. Bruno was a member of the Saxon nobility who at an early age became the chaplain of Emperor Otto III. The Emperor was much attached to the gifted young priest, but Bruno left the imperial court to become a Benedictine monk and a missioner among the savage Pechenegs of the Russian steppes.

Saint Bruno passed through Kiev and Vladimir detained the German monk for a month in his capital, seeking to dissuade him from his perilous mission. In a dream, God revealed to Vladimir that He desired the evangelization of the Pechenegs. Then the Kievan ruler gave the missioner a Russian bishop as assistant and his own royal son to serve as interpreter among the nomads. Vladimir himself accompanied Bruno during the two days' journey to the Kievan frontier. The Grand Prince saw through tear-dimmed eyes the wild country of the Pechenegs. "Once more, dear friend, I beg you to have a care for your own life!" he called out.

Saint Bruno's only answer was: "May God open to you the gates of Paradise, even as you have opened to me the way to the barbarians." Then the German apostle set out across the steppes with his companions, while Prince Vladimir watched until he could see only dark specks moving on the flat horizon.

Later Saint Bruno returned safely to Kiev. He announced to his overjoyed royal friend the baptism of some thirty Perchenegs. No better evidence of Prince Vladimir's attitude toward Rome could be had than his loving veneration for Saint Bruno, the Latin missioner.[9]

So passed the fruitful years after Vladimir's conversion. The Russian Chronicle summarizes this period of his reign in the beautiful words: "Thus did Christianity diffuse her light over Russia, like the rising sun, with progressively increasing splendor. And Vladimir rejoiced thereat, and was liberal towards the poor and afflicted, and distributed his gifts among all the people."[10] In the year 1015 Saint Vladimir went to an apostle's reward.

After Prince Vladimir's death, the succession to the Kievan throne was disputed. Svyatopolk, the eldest heir, ordered the murder of his brothers, Boris and Gleb, beloved by the people. The two young princes suffered death without offering any resistance, in order to avert civil strife in the dear land of Russia. The Russian clergy and people requested successfully the canonization of Boris and Gleb, because the royal brothers had imitated Christ in His kenosis, His voluntary humiliation and sacrificial death. In the end final victory in the disputed succession rested with another of Vladimir's sons, the gifted Yaroslav (1019–1054).

The Charlemagne of Russia

Yaroslav the Great, one of Russia's ablest rulers, placed his realm under the special protection of the Blessed Virgin Mary. From the time of that ancient dedication, Christian Russia manifested ardent devotion to the Mother of God, and miraculous icons of the Virgin have been associated with the most stirring events of Russian history.

Yaroslav was in frequent communication with the Holy See and with the German Emperor, Henry III. He gave valuable support to the royal apostle, Saint Olav, in the evangelization of Norway. The Russian Grand Prince was united by family alliances with the Catholic royal houses of Poland, Hungary, Germany, Norway, and France. The most brilliant of all those marriages was that of Yaroslav's daughter, Anne, with King Henry I of France. Today Queen Anne's Slavonic Bible is preserved in Reims Cathedral. Her son, Count Hugh the Great, was among the heroes of the First Crusade.[11]

In the last years of his reign Yaroslav showed a tendency to act independently of the Patriarch of Constantinople. In 1051, when the Metropolitan See of Russia became vacant, Yaroslav authorized his bishops to elect Metropolitan Hilarion, the first prelate of Russian origin to hold that post. The Grand Prince refused to seek the Greek Patriarch's approval of Hilarion's election. Yaroslav may have been aware that, just at that time, Patriarch Cerularius was fomenting a division between the Eastern Churches and Rome.

The long reign of Yaroslav was comparatively peaceful, and he was successful in the wars that he fought. To a still greater degree he merited well of Russia by his ceaseless efforts to increase the culture of his people. Under Yaroslav's direction his clergy compiled a Church law, the *Russkaya Pravda,* based on Byzantine secular codes. The Grand Prince engaged the services of architects, artists, and singers from Constantinople. The superb Russian church music began to develop. Yaroslav provided for the copying and translating of Greek manuscripts, of which he made a permanent library in a church that he had built in Kiev.

The early Christians of Russia knew the Bible chiefly through the liturgy, and many of them could recite the Psalms by heart. Among the works of the Greek Fathers, those of Saint John Chrysostom and of Saint John Damascene were preferred. Calendars of the lives of the saints were eagerly and extensively read. Some monks in the Kievan Monastery of the Caves were beginning to labor on the earliest Russian annals.

In 1054 Yaroslav, the Charlemagne of Russia, died. Perhaps the only untoward event of his rule was his establishment of an unduly complicated order of succession. The ensuing internecine wars of his descendants were destined to hasten the ultimate breakup of Kievan Russia.

Russia and the Schism

At the time of Yaroslav's death, the contumacious Patriarch Cerularius of Constantinople brought to a head the Greek Schism, which had been developing for centuries before a lasting separation from Rome took place. In 1054 the Russian Church had no part in the Greek Schism. Unlike proud Constantinople, young Kiev had no reasons for jealousy of the See of Peter; moreover, Kievan Russia had many and close ties with Western Europe. Consequently, the relations between Russia and Rome were preserved intact for about a century and a half after Constantinople had separated from the Holy See.

Izyaslav, the eldest son of the deceased Yaroslav, had much trouble in ascending his throne. He thereupon turned in all confidence to the Holy See, seeking the intervention of Pope Gregory VII in favor of his succession. It is impossible to suppose that Izyaslav would have appealed to the Pope in this manner, if his subjects had not been friendly to Rome.

Prince Izyaslav had great veneration for Theodosius, the holy Abbot of Kiev's Monastery of the Caves. The Grand Prince confessed his sins to his friend, and he considered it a privilege to share the monastery's humble fare of "boiled grain, bread, and fish." Saint Theodosius died in 1074. Soon afterwards his life was recorded by the celebrated Nestor, also a monk of the Monastery of the Caves. Nestor gives us precious glimpses of ancient Russia, such as a vivid description of Kievan pilgrims returning from the Holy Land.[12]

Gathering Darkness

After the death of the Russian-born Metropolitan Hilarion in 1055, Patriarch Cerularius of Constantinople hastened to restore the former relations with the Kievan Church. He sent a Greek prelate to Kiev as Metropolitan, and a propaganda campaign of hatred against the Latin Christians was forthwith inaugurated among the Russians.

Yaroslav's descendants had to do battle against the Polovtsy, a powerful Asiatic people who had succeeded the defeated Pechenegs on the lower Dnieper. The beautiful city of Kiev became a prize clutched at by a constant succession of brief rulers, and the fighting companies of the contesting princes were a scourge to the land. Papal legates continued to arrive in Russia, but the ceaseless civil wars among the princes made long range political and religious planning impossible. As Kiev weakened, an increasing number of Russians fell into the hands of the heathen Polovtsy and were enslaved. Yet because of the glowing patriotism of the ordinary people of Kiev, the chivalrous fight against hopeless odds was long maintained.

From the middle of the eleventh century the population of

the Kievan area began to migrate northeastward along the Desna River, a tributary of the Dnieper. They settled in dense thickets, the surest way of escaping the attacks of the nomads. As the Russian refugees laboriously cleared small patches in the forests, they came into peaceful contact with the scattered Finns. In time intermarriage did its work, and the bright Slavonic nature acquired new strength from this blending with the stolid Finns. The vague pagan beliefs of the Finns could not long resist the impact of Russian Christianity, so the faith of the migrants ultimately prevailed among the Finnish aborigines.

Cultural Afterglow

While Kiev held the supremacy in the Russian State, it spread civilization far and wide over the whole area. The Chronicles were continued, and the twelfth century Kievan Chronicle compares favorably with the best examples of medieval history in Western Europe. The masterpiece of ancient Russian literature, the powerful *Tale of the Host of Igor,* was written by an anonymous poet shortly after Prince Igor's defeat at the hands of the Polovtsy in 1185.

The real creative power of the genius of old Russia was visible in her art and architecture, rather than in her literature. Early Christian Russia had a golden age of painting, before the static tendencies of the national Church standardized the icon. There was an indigenous and very attractive architecture, still to be seen in the wooden churches of northwestern Russia and in the brick ones built along similar lines.[13]

Although Christianity continued to grow in Russia throughout the Kievan period, many of the higher clergy were Greeks, who had little understanding of the language or of the customs of their flocks. Moreover, the bishops had too few priests at their command to provide for the needs of the huge dioceses of Russia. Though the monks commanded the veneration of the people, monasticism in Russia never developed the rich diversity of works that it manifested in Western Christendom. For the Russian people Christianity was primarily neither a system of doctrines nor an institution, but a way of life. They paid less attention to discipline and order than Western Christians, but rejoiced in the beauty of their rich liturgy and in a profound sense of God's mercy and forgiveness.

The Slow Sundering

During the period of the breakup of the Kievan realm, Russia was drawn gradually and almost insensibly into the shadows of the Byzantine Schism. The Russian Church could not escape the influence of its Greek prelates; nevertheless, because there had been no direct misunderstanding with Rome, friendly relations with the Holy See were maintained until the early years of the thirteenth century. Thirty years after the Greek Schism, Pope Urban II sent a delegation to Russia with the relics of Saint Nicholas of Bari. The people of Kiev received the papal envoys with veneration and great rejoicing.[14]

Russian bishops of the southwestern principalities were more than once consecrated by the nearest Latin archbishop until the end of the Kievan period. In the eleventh century or at the beginning of the twelfth, a Latin monastery was established on the Volkhov River. The Russian liturgical books and chants of the close of the twelfth century still included the name of the Pope.

In spite of the foregoing evidences of friendship between Russia and Rome, the corroding influence of Greek hatred of the Latins had then already been long at work in the Kievan realm. In the Byzantine Empire itself, dislike of the Latins changed into active hatred with the arrival of the Western Crusaders, who only too often treated the Greeks with roughness and contempt. The extreme limit of bitterness was reached when, in 1204, by a shameful deviation from their avowed ideals, the Crusaders occupied Constantinople and established the short-lived Latin Empire.[15]

The Greek prelates in Russia did not fail to describe to their flocks all the abominations of the Crusaders against the Eastern Church. Because the Russians attached such immense importance to the externals of religion, they heard with horror that the Latin ceremonies differed in various respects from their own. By the early years of the thirteenth century misled Russia was ripe for participation in the Eastern Schism.

In 1320 Pope John XXII wrote as follows to a Dominican missioner at Kiev: "Unfortunately, the clergy and people of the Church of Kiev have had no real pastor for the past one hundred years and more, because of the schism which malignant influences brought about." This statement of the Holy Father would place the event of Russia's definite separation from the Roman Church at the beginning of the thirteenth century.[16]

Spiritual and Physical Isolation

At the opening of the thirteenth century the Russian colonization resulting from the breakup of the Kievan realm had reached the region of the Middle Volga. Then the advance of the Russians was violently halted by the northern edge of the crescent of Mongolian conquest. In their turn the Tartars, the terrible warriors of Genghis Khan, swept over Russia towards the riches of Western Europe. The princes of southern Russia were not supported in their crucial struggle against the Tartars by the new northern principalities. The southern princes went down in bloody defeat on the Kalka River in 1228.

In 1237 the Tartar general, Batu, laid waste the northern principalities of Russia. The turn of Kiev came in 1240. When Friar John of Plano Carpini passed by the ruined Mother of Russian Cities, on his way to the desert headquarters of the

Great Khan at distant Karakorum, he saw on all sides pyramids of skulls and heaps of human bones.[17]

Russia had already been cut off by schism from the plenitude of Christianity. Now the Tartar domination would sever her from the civilization of Constantinople and from her own southwestern provinces. The Russian regions of Volhynia and Galicia began to lead a separate existence, and later they came under the rule of Lithuania and Poland.

There remained to the new Russia in the isolated northern forests only the splendor of the Eastern Liturgy. The suffering people clung to their Church with a passionate love, and Russian religion became intensely national and inextricably interwoven with Russian patriotism.

Footnotes to Chapter One

[1] G. F. Maclear, *Conversion of the West: The Slavs,* p. 94 f.
[2] *Cambridge Medieval History.* Vol. IV, pp. 219–22.
[3] D. Mackenzie Wallace, *Russia,* p. 184.
[4] George Vernadsky, *A History of Russia,* p. 28.
[5] John Maynard, *Russia in Flux,* p. 1.
[6] *Nestor's Chronicle,* in Leo Wiener's *Anthology of Russian Literature.* Vol. I, pp. 65–71.
[7] Nicolas Zernov, *The Russians and Their Church,* pp. 7–19.
[8] Joseph B. Koncevicius, *Russia's Attitude Towards Union with Rome,* pp. 28–30.
[9] Paul Pierling, *La Russie et le Saint-Siège.* Vol. I, pp. X f.
[10] G. F. Maclear, *op. cit.,* p. 107.
[11] Helen Iswolsky, *Soul of Russia,* p. 5.
[12] G. P. Fedotov, editor, *A Treasury of Russian Spirituality,* pp. 11–49.
[13] George Vernadsky, *Kievan Russia,* pp. 256–63.
[14] Horace K. Mann, *The Lives of the Popes in the Middle Ages.* Vol. VI, p. 164.
[15] Louis Bréhier, *L'Eglise et l'Orient au Moyen Age: Les Croisades,* pp. 150–76.
[16] Joseph B. Koncevicius, *op. cit.,* pp. 54 f.
[17] Bernard Pares, *A History of Russia,* p. 53.

CHAPTER TWO

Basil Condemns the "Ravening Wolf"

THE TARTAR invasion of Russia caused apprehension throughout Europe and Pope Innocent IV ordered that means of repelling the Mongolian menace be carefully considered at the First Council of Lyons, assembled in 1245. A Russian archbishop by the name of Peter, an eyewitness of the Tartar devastations, gave first-hand information to the members of the council.

Batu, the grandson of Genghis Khan, built Serai, his populous capital, on one of the arms of the Lower Volga. The Russian princes were obliged to acknowledge the supremacy of the Tartar khan at Serai, and to ask of him confirmation in their office of provincial ruler. Some of the unfortunate Russian princes, indeed, were ordered to trek across the deserts of Central Asia and to do homage to the Great Khan at Karakorum, south of Lake Baikal.[1]

Under the Tartar Yoke

The Tartars permitted the vanquished to retain their land, their language, their courts of justice, and their other institutions; but Russia was squeezed dry by the exactions of the conquerors' taxgatherers. Those unable to pay the capitation tax became slaves. The Russians had to furnish a military contingent to the Tartars, and at this time Russian military organization and equipment became Oriental.

Only their Church kept alive among the Russian people a stubbornly heroic national consciousness. It was a dark literary age, but Russian art recovered rapidly from the decline caused by the Tartar invasion. The master icon-painter of the period was Andrew Rublev, a monk of the renowned Trinity Monastery in the vicinity of Moscow, who died about the year 1427.[2]

Amid so much suffering and desolation, the heaviest penalty of all was paid by the Russian peasant colonizers of the northern forests, because the Tartar yoke favored the development of serfdom. The peasants fell into increasing dependence upon the boyars, who offered them a measure of security and aid in the cultivation of the poor soil of the forest zone. Already at that early date, the Russian peasants were on their way to becoming the most oppressed class in a formidable autocracy.

The Tartars realized that the Orthodox clergy had the power to calm or to arouse their flocks, so the Asiatic conquerors protected the Russian Church and granted her a considerable measure of freedom from secular authority. It was only after the Tartars of Serai had embraced the religion of the Prophet that a single one of their rulers, Uzbek, attempted unsuccessfully in the fourteenth century to propagate the tenets of Islam among the Russians.

At this same period, under the leadership of Saint Sergius of Radonezh, pioneers of the great monastic revival left the towns and took refuge in the virgin forests. But disciples soon gathered in the vicinity of the hermitages, and new monasteries sprang up. Eventually peasant communities took shape around these monasteries. Thus, unwittingly, the hermit-monks had initiated an irresistible movement of Christian colonization in the wilderness. In less than three centuries the north of European Russia, far into the Arctic regions, was nominally conquered for Christ. It is true, of course, that some isolated Arctic tribes were never evangelized.

Among the Tartars of Serai, in southern Russia, Catholic missions flourished for more than two generations. The missioners were members of the Franciscan and Dominican Orders. The bishopric of Caffa, founded in the Crimea by Pope John XXII (1316–1334), became a great center of Latin influence. Converts were made even among the members of the Tartar royal family. After the middle of the fourteenth century the Black Death almost wiped out the Catholic missioners of the steppes, but reinforcements were sent. At the close of that century an increasing number of the Christians in the region of the Caucasus were being brought into union with Rome.[3]

Catholics Considered as National Enemies

At the time of the Tartar invasion Russia received no aid from Latin Catholics. On the contrary, both Swedes and Teutonic Knights assailed the stricken people at this crucial moment. These Catholic enemies were defeated by the Russian national hero, Prince Alexander Nevsky of Vladimir-Suzdal, who was later canonized by the Orthodox Church. Toward the middle of the thirteenth century Pope Innocent IV sent delegates to Alexander Nevsky, in an attempt to persuade the Russian leader to unite himself with Rome. Prince Alexander would not adhere to the religion of his country's enemies. He told the papal envoys that he rejected the "teaching of the Latins." [4]

After the period of Alexander Nevsky, Russian hostility toward Catholicism as the religion of the aggressive Westerners grew apace. Russian princes who formed alliances with the Lithuanians or the Poles were considered as traitors to Orthodoxy and to their country. Virtually no intercourse in spiritual matters existed between the new Russia of the forests and the Holy See.

The social, cultural, and religious centers of Russia proper were now much farther from Western Europe than they had been in the days of the Kievan realm. In 1325, after Moscow had risen to political supremacy, Metropolitan Peter moved to that city, and his successors remained there. The physical isolation of Russia from Rome was accentuated by the intervention between the two of a new power, that of Lithuania. The efforts of the Holy See to reach the Russians remained of no avail, and in his apostolic frustration Pope John XXII called them "perverse schismatics." [5]

In the fourteenth and the fifteenth centuries, Russian writers began to compile books from Greek sources in which inconsequential and absurd charges against the Latin Church were repeated in profusion. It was recorded with horror that the Latins shaved their beards, that Roman Catholic bishops wore rings, and that Western Europeans ate from the same dishes with dogs!

The Russians became so prejudiced against the Westerners that they no longer considered baptism according to the Latin rite as valid. When a Roman Catholic joined the Russian Church, he was rebaptized according to the Greek rite. In Russia no Roman Catholic could hold any public office. Friendships with Westerners were out of the question. Moscow even disapproved of Novgorod's mercantile dealings with German Catholics.

The City on the Moskva River

Among all the Russian princes vying with one another for the favor of the Mongolian conquerors, in order to be appointed Grand Prince and deputy taxgatherer by the Tartars, the rulers of Moscow were the most cunning and the most persevering. In time, the Tartars of Serai allowed the Muscovite princes to become their chief lieutenants in collecting the tribute. Thus the astute princes of Moscow rose to power, and made use of their privileged position to absorb gradually all the other Russian principalities into their own. After the Grand Princes of Moscow had brought the other principalities under their sway, they treated their boyars as menials. When the nobles entered the presence of the Muscovite Grand Prince, they prostrated themselves repeatedly in Oriental fashion.

The then unimportant settlement of Moscow, on the Moskva River, was first surrounded with wooden walls in 1156. At first it was an appanage of younger sons, but Moscow was favorably situated for expansion. By the river system of Central Russia the young settlement had access to Kiev, to Novgorod, and to the Caspian. Moscow attracted settlers as Russian colonization moved along the rivers, and the trade of the expanding town began to flourish.

Free peasants voluntarily entered the service of the Muscovite princes, because in the insecure Russia of those days labor would go wherever it could obtain protection and good conditions of work. Meanwhile, the Muscovite princes neglected no means, fair or foul, of patiently uniting all Russia under their sway. Under the rule of those scheming "gathering princes" was formed a people long-suffering and resigned, yet also enterprising and resourceful.

The great prelates of a Church that was not yet the minion of the State perceived that alone of all the Russian princes, those of Muscovy were equal to the stern destiny of forming a nation under the very eyes of the conquerors and then of casting off the Tartar yoke. So the metropolitans made their home in Moscow, and gave to the city the immense strength of becoming the religious as well as the political heart of Russia.

On the Frontiers of Muscovy

The ancient merchant city of Novgorod had been saved from the Tartar invaders by its surrounding marshes. This important commercial center had long gloried in many democratic institutions. It had extended its sway over a vast northern hinterland, reaching to the northeastern corner of Europe and sparsely inhabited by Finns or other alien tribes. Novgorod became an intermediary between the new mercantile Europe and the city's own enormous hinterland resources. But now the princes of expanding Muscovy were casting ambitious eyes upon the riches of Novgorod, and a power which could control the food supplies of the Middle Volga could always subdue the proud townspeople of Novgorod by starving them out.

The city of Pskov, long a frontier town of Russia, was governed on the same democratic principles as Novgorod. Pskov realized those principles better in practice, because it did not have such sharp contrasts of wealth and poverty and its code of justice was very humane.

In the twelfth century northwestern Russia had included the territory of present-day Latvia and Estonia. Those regions were then under the rule of the prince of Polotsk. Latin missioners evangelized this section, at first with the permission of the Russian prince. When the Catholics in those parts had increased in power, they organized the independent State of Livonia. After that, unfriendly relations between Livonia and the rulers of Polotsk arose; the Russians did not approve of the Latin rite used by the Livonians.[6]

In the fourteenth century Volhynia and Kiev passed under the rule of the new State of Lithuania. Galicia was later annexed to Poland. In 1386 Poland and Lithuania were united under one king, and the Russians of the water road became subject to Latin Christians. This event was the signal of a standing quarrel between Muscovy and Poland-Lithuania, certain to lead to ceaseless wars.

Two separate metropolitans were constituted for Russia about the year 1415. The Metropolitan of Kiev ruled the Russians under Polish sway, while the Metropolitan of Moscow ruled the people of Russia proper. The influence of Moscow was in favor of the schism. The Metropolitans of Kiev, on the other hand, kept their subjects longer in union with Rome. But in the sixteenth century Metropolitan Job of Moscow was consecrated Patriarch of the whole Russian Church. After that time schism became the order of the day.[7]

Early "Gatherers of the Russian Land"

Metropolitan Peter, the first head of the Russian Church to reside in Moscow, gave wise and patriotic counsel to Prince Ivan Moneybag (1328–1340). Metropolitan Peter foretold the future greatness of Moscow, saying, "Her hands will go forth over the shoulders of her enemies."

The Tartars were so pleased with Simeon the Proud (1340–1353), that they "put all the other princes in Simeon's hands." During the reign of this Grand Prince, the beloved, young Saint Sergius led a strong monastic revival. The great Monastery of the Trinity was built at Radonezh, on the site of the saint's hermitage in the forest some forty miles north of Moscow. The Monastery of the Trinity was soon able to make many new foundations. Saint Sergius was favored by heavenly visions. Today the Catholic Church, as well as the Orthodox, recognizes Sergius of Radonezh as a saint.

During the rule of Ivan II (1353–1359), the Tartars gave the sovereign of Moscow the right of justice over the other

Russian princes. The chivalrous Dmitry of the Don (1359–1389) was the first of the Muscovite princes to flaunt the Tartar yoke. Dmitry had as close adviser Metropolitan Alexis, a man of strong and deep spirituality. Alexis constantly exhorted his sovereign to remove the yoke from the Russian land. A series of skirmishes and military actions led up to the fierce battle of Kulikovo (1380), a meadow on the upper reaches of the Don River.

Before setting out for the battle, Dmitry sought the blessing of Saint Sergius. The renowned mystic gave the Grand Prince two monks to fight at his side. The people were electrified by the news that "Seekers of Silence" had left the peace of their cells to do battle for the land of Russia. The clash at Kulikovo was tremendous, but a superb charge of the Russian cavalry won the day. Although Mongolian domination was to last for another century, the victory at Kulikovo showed the Russians that the Tartars were not invincible. The people venerated both Dmitry of the Don and Saint Sergius as national heroes and builders of Muscovy.

While Basil I (1389–1425) was Grand Prince, a new Asiatic world-conqueror arose, Timur the Great. Timur entered Russian territory in 1395. Basil marched out to meet the terrible Mongol, and he sent in haste for the wonder-working icon of the Holy Virgin of Vladimir. On the day that the icon reached Moscow came the glad tidings that Timur had passed on to other conquests.[8]

A Dismayed Muscovite Ruler

Basil II (1425–1462) was utterly confused by the current attitude of the Greek Emperor and the Greek Patriarch. It was reported that they actually desired union with the Pope of Rome. The mere thought of such a reunion filled the Russian Grand Prince with dismay and displeasure. Basil II desired to govern the Russian Church without the "meddling interference" of any Latin Pontiff.

It was quite true that in his supreme distress Emperor John VIII Paleologus had turned to Pope Eugenius IV (1431–1447). Only the Byzantine capital was then still holding out against the Turks; and the Greek ruler was willing to have the Eastern Churches unite with Rome, if only he could obtain military aid from the West against the dreaded infidels. The venerable Patriarch Joseph likewise desired union with Rome, though for more supernatural motives. In 1434 John Paleologus sent delegates to the Council of Basel, to make preliminary arrangements for a reunion council. Outstanding among the Emperor's envoys was the learned, pious, and patriotic monk Isidore, well known at the Greek court.

In his dire need John Paleologus hoped to secure the military assistance of the Russians. For the sake of greater over-all harmony the Emperor thought that it would be expedient to win over the Muscovites to the idea of reunion of the churches. At that time Basil II had already designated for the office of Russian Metropolitan his trusted adviser, Bishop Jonas of Riazan. But the zeal for the union of the Churches shown by Isidore at Basel made it clear that the venerated monk would be an ideal instrument for the task of propagating the concept of reunion among the Muscovites. Patriarch Joseph accordingly appointed Isidore Metropolitan of Russia.

Isidore set out for Moscow early in the year 1437, knowing little about the peculiar political and religious conditions in Muscovy. The Russian Grand Prince was naturally displeased by the rejection of Bishop Jonas, his own candidate, but the prestige of Constantinople was still so great in Muscovy that Basil resigned himself to the acceptance of Isidore. Metropolitan Isidore made a powerful impression on his new subjects by the scope of his learning, but almost at once he began to talk about a Church assembly in Italy, to which the Patriarch desired Russia to send representatives.

Basil was dumbfounded; now the Greeks were asking the Russians to discuss theology with Western heretics! In the end the Grand Prince felt obliged to yield to the inexplicable wishes of the Greek Patriarch, but he gave a stern warning to Isidore: "Come back to us with the ancient faith of Vladimir. Have great care not to change that faith in the slightest degree, for any innovation would be displeasing to us." [9]

The Russians Are Scandalized

Isidore and his suite of about a hundred persons journeyed to Lübeck, and from that commercial city they made their way southward through Germany. Great was the amazement of the Muscovites at the architectural and mechanical wonders of Western Europe. In August, 1438, the wayfarers arrived at Ferrara. The council had already begun its sessions, over which Pope Eugenius IV presided in person.

Before the end of the year pestilence broke out in Ferrara, and the council then transferred its sessions to Florence, the brilliant court of the Medici. Prominent among the Greek delegates was the learned and upright Metropolitan Bessarion, who took a leading part in the theological discussions. The doctrinal decisions of the Council of Florence have remained as the basis for union between Rome and the Eastern Churches, a union founded upon oneness in faith and diversity in rites.

The promulgation of the bull of union took place on July 6, 1439. Meanwhile, the feelings of Isidore's Russian companions had been outraged by their Metropolitan's tireless efforts for the success of the union of the churches. Pope Eugenius IV made Isidore his legate and entrusted to him the task of gaining Moscow's approval of the decisions of the Council of Florence. In December, 1439 the Holy Father raised Bessarion and Isidore to the cardinalate.

Isidore did not reach the Russian capital until March, 1441.

He went in procession to the cathedral, preceded by the Latin cross, with the figure of Christ in relief which so shocked the devout and ignorant Muscovites. At the moment of the liturgical commemorations, the scandalized Grand Prince heard the name of Pope Eugenius IV, instead of that of the Patriarch of Constantinople. The climax came after the Mass, when the Metropolitan promulgated the bull of union. Basil II cried out that Isidore was a ravening wolf, instead of a good shepherd. The Grand Prince had the Metropolitan thrown into the dungeons of the Chudov Monastery.

An assembly of Russian prelates condemned Isidore as a treacherous heretic, and Basil repudiated the terms of the union without the slightest hesitation. Fortunately the condemned Isidore escaped from prison. Rejected by the Slavs, the cardinal-legate made his way to Italy. There the brave champion of the union of the Churches died on April 27, 1463.[10]

After Isidore had fled into exile, the Church in Muscovy remained without a Metropolitan for some years. In 1448 the Grand Prince and an assembly of the Russian prelates appointed Bishop Jonas as Metropolitan. From then onward the Russian Church no longer recognized dependence on the Byzantine Patriarch.

Political Developments

Constantinople, the proud "second Rome," fell to the Turks on May 29, 1453, and the last of the Byzantine Emperors was slain on the ramparts of his vanquished capital. Constantine XII, the eightieth Roman Emperor since Constantine the Great, died in heroic glory, in union with the Holy See and the Catholic Church. A terrible carnage followed the Turkish victory.

After the fall of Constantinople successive Popes sought on all sides Christian allies against the Turks. Muscovy was reputed to have a strong army, but the Popes were hampered in their dealings with the Russians by lack of knowledge of the true state of affairs in Muscovy. Already Russia was an enigma to Western Europe. Moreover, the rulers of Poland hampered the establishment of relations between Muscovy and the Holy See. Professed champions of the Catholic religion as they were, the Poles yet dreaded to see their "barbaric" enemy gain strength by becoming Westernized.

The conquered territories of sundered Russia did not cease to strain toward reunion with their countrymen, and Moscow clamored with increasing truculence for their restitution. The permanently bitter enmity between the two Slavic nations manifested itself periodically in open warfare, and proved a major obstacle to any softening of Russian hearts toward the "Pope of the Poles." In addition, the Latin clergy and nobles in Poland-Lithuania regarded the Russian Orthodox as being on a lower social plane than themselves. The Russians resented this assumption of superiority, and mutual bad feeling was harmful to reunion of the Churches.[11]

At this time the once-mighty Tartars of Serai had been so weakened by internal dissensions that they were beaten off at all points when they appeared before Moscow in 1451. Prince Ivan, the able son of Basil II, defeated the ruler of Galicia. Galicia with all its dependencies was then joined to Muscovy. During this reign Muscovy advanced steadily into the vast hinterland empire of the merchant city of Novgorod. The advance was one of peaceful colonization, and Novgorod had no way of halting it. The Novgorodians knew that Basil II could at any time reduce them to starvation, merely by barring the passage of the Middle Volga.

The Grand Prince who had been so scandalized by the "heresy" of Metropolitan Isidore died in 1462, leaving his much strengthened throne to Ivan III, often called the Great. The domain of Muscovy had by then swelled to fifteen thousand square miles.

Emergence of a Messianic Ideal

While a proud sense of their political destiny was deepening the patriotism of the Muscovites, they were gripped also by the dawning vision of a grandiose spiritual mission. This concept of predestined spiritual leadership was henceforth to become an essential part of the national psychology, and it would increase immeasurably the difficulty of Russia's recognition of a Vicar of Christ in Rome.

The fall of Constantinople was looked upon in Russia as a just punishment by the Almighty for the "sin of union." Constantinople, the splendid but unfaithful second Rome, was now prostrate under the heels of the infidels. In all the world there remained but one great Orthodox sovereign, the ruler of Muscovy. Was he not destined to assume henceforth the role of the fallen Byzantine Emperors, and had not the appointed time arrived for Holy Mother Moscow to shine before the nations as the third Rome?

Some years later the monk Philotheus, abbot of a monastery in Pskov, would give striking expression to the Russian dream in a letter to the grandson of Basil II. Philotheus wrote: "The Church of ancient Rome fell because of Apollinarian heresy. As to the second Rome, it has been hewn down by the axes of the Ishmaelites. But this third Rome, the Holy Apostolic Church, under thy mighty rule shines throughout the entire world more brightly than the sun. . . . Two Romes have fallen, but the third stands and no fourth can ever be." [12]

Footnotes to Chapter Two

[1] Alexandre Eck, *Le Moyen Age Russe,* pp. 37–42.
[2] Paul Miliukov, *Outlines of Russian Culture.* Part III, p. 36.
[3] Kenneth Scott Latourette, *A History of the Expansion of Christianity.* Vol. II, pp. 334 f.
[4] Helen Iswolsky, *Soul of Russia,* p. 15.
[5] Augustinus Theiner, *Vetera Monumenta Poloniae et Lithuaniae.* Vol. I, p. 131.

[6] A. J. Turgenev, *Historica Russiae Monumenta.* Vol. I, p. 13.

[7] Horace K. Mann, *The Lives of the Popes in the Middle Ages.* Vol. XIV, p. 205.

[8] Wirt Gerrare, *The Story of Moscow,* p. 26.

[9] Paul Pierling, *La Russie et le Saint-Siège.* Vol. I, p. 22.

[10] A. M. Ammann, *Storia della Chiesa Russa,* pp. 124 f.

[11] Joseph B. Koncevicius, *Russia's Attitude Towards Union With* Rome, p. 147.

[12] Alexandre Eck, *op. cit.,* pp. 440 f.

CHAPTER THREE

The Third Rome

THE THIRD Ivan was cold, imperious, and calculating. He did not hesitate to punish and to torture his boyars, even those of the highest rank. Ivan III was but adding another, similar chapter to the history of much-suffering medieval Russia. The great Russian historian, Klyuchevsky, wrote: "The Muscovite State was formed painfully and slowly. We now can scarcely understand and still less feel what sacrifices of the people's welfare it cost; how it pressed down on the existence of the individual." [1]

Ivan III (1462–1505) had much to accomplish in order to strengthen his poor, backward, landlocked, and isolated realm. In the years between 1465 and 1488 he absorbed Novgorod and its immense hinterland without having to wage any extensive campaign. Ivan had his party within the city itself, and he knew how to profit by the selfish quarrels of Novgorod's ruling classes.

In 1477, after the Novgorodians had appealed for aid to King Casimir IV of Poland, Ivan marched on the city, executed his principal enemies, and then transported hundreds of the inhabitants to the Middle Volga. The Grand Prince repeated this drastic measure during successive years, and in the same arbitrary and wholesale manner he moved families from Moscow into Novgorodian territory. The ancient glory of Novgorod had been trampled into the dust.

Vaulting Hopes of Reunion

In Rome, Pope Pius II had given generous shelter to Thomas Paleologus, the brother of the last Emperor of Constantinople. Thomas, a widower, died in the Eternal City in 1465, after having recommended to the care of Cardinal Bessarion his two sons and his young daughter, Zoe. The great Greek Churchman made every effort to educate his wards as stanch Catholics. Princess Zoe developed into a beautiful young woman, apparently much attached to the Catholic Church. All Western Europe was thrilled when, in 1469, the remote ruler of mysterious Muscovy asked the Byzantine princess in marriage.

At that time a clever Italian adventurer, John-Baptist Volpe, and his nephew, Antonio Gislardi, were among the few foreigners living in Moscow. Ivan made use of Volpe as his envoy in negotiating with Rome for the marriage with Zoe Paleologus. The wily Volpe told Pope Sixtus IV (1471–1484) that Ivan III was eager for the reunion of the Churches and desired that a papal legate should be sent to Moscow. There was no truth in the Italian adventurer's fabrications.

The Pope gave Zoe rich presents and a dowry of six thousand ducats. He also provided a suitable escort of Greeks and Italians to accompany her to Moscow. Among the Italians was a papal legate, Bishop Anthony Bonumbre. It was November, 1472, when the Greek bride arrived in Russia, and Moscow wore a wintry mantle of snow. The city's low, wooden houses must have surprised a princess accustomed to the splendors of Renaissance Italy.

A few days later, the Russian Metropolitan united Ivan III and his bride according to the Eastern rite. In Muscovy Zoe was called Sophia, and with a new name she appears to have assumed a new personality. Showing herself an ardent adherent of the Orthodox Church, Sophia from then on rejected the teachings of her Roman benefactors.

As for the papal legate, Anthony Bonumbre, he remained in Moscow for about eleven weeks. He was certainly a skilled diplomat, and returned to Italy loaded with presents. On his arrival in Rome, he no doubt informed the Pope that the attitude of the Russians toward the Holy See was not at all as it had been described by Volpe. Later, Bishop Bonumbre was again delegated to Muscovy on a special mission.

In 1473, Gislardi, Volpe's nephew, arrived in Rome and solemnly assured the Pope that the Russians wished to recognize him as the legitimate successor of Saint Peter. Sixtus IV was resolved not to neglect any opportunity of an understanding with the schismatics, so he gave Gislardi important messages for Ivan III. Nothing came of these messages, for the simple reason that the whole affair was a hoax originating in the scheming brain of Volpe.[2]

The Tartar Yoke Is Broken

All the while, Ivan III had been steadily gathering in the appanages of his princely relatives in northern and central Russia. He was biding his time in his dealings with the Tartars of Serai. But after he had married the proud Sophia, she would often egg him on with the complaint, "How long am I to be the slave of the Tartars?" [3]

Ivan accordingly took up a position of open challenge. The surprised Mongols allied themselves with Casimir IV of Poland and marched on Moscow. But the Russian ruler was meanwhile enmeshing the Tartars in the cunning web of his devious diplomacy. In 1480 the confused Asiatics retreated of their own accord. Shortly afterwards, the power of the Tartars of Serai was permanently broken by the recently established khanate of Crimea, with which Ivan prudently formed friendly relations. In this tortuous and inglorious way, the third Ivan freed Russia from the Tartar yoke.

At this period Lithuania was making attempts to unite Orthodox princes and their subjects to Rome. The Orthodox princes who were nearest to Muscovite territory hastened to transfer themselves to the allegiance of Ivan III. The latter, in company with his Tartar allies of the Crimea, proceeded to harass the frontiers of Lithuania and seized some fortresses.

Lithuania's Grand Duke Alexander was not warlike. In 1495 he hoped to cement peace with Ivan by marrying the Russian ruler's daughter, Helena. Helena brought with her from Moscow some schismatic priests. She eventually succeeded in having them promoted to high positions, in which they were able to exercise a strong influence over the Lithuanian people in favor of the schism.

Five years after his marriage with Helena, Duke Alexander was seized with religious scruples. He submitted his case to Pope Alexander VI (1492–1503), who said that Helena must become a Catholic. Ivan and Sophia sternly forbade their daughter to take this step. "Rather death than apostasy," wrote the Muscovite ruler.[4]

Alexander's breach of promise concerning Helena's religion furnished an excellent excuse for renewing hostilities. From 1500 onward Ivan continued war with his son-in-law, though on one occasion Pope Alexander VI succeeded in patching up an insecure peace between the two rulers, using the king of Hungary as an intermediary. Each time that Ivan negotiated with Lithuania, he retained all the territory that he had annexed.

Reflected Rays of the Renaissance

Ivan III enlisted in his service the talents of some of the Greeks and the Italians who had accompanied his wife to Moscow. Great Italian architects, among whom the most renowned was Aristotle Fioraventi, transformed the appearance of the Muscovite capital by uniting Renaissance art with ancient Byzantine and Russian motifs. They built the crenelated walls and the elegant gates of the Kremlin, and famous cathedrals within the enclosure.

Aided chiefly by the Greeks, the Muscovite ruler established diplomatic relations with the outside world. The Russian ambassadors soon showed a high degree of cunning skill. In the courts of Western Europe they were great sticklers for etiquette and always strove to have precedence over the envoys of other nations. Because the Grand Prince was most anxious to obtain the services of foreign architects, artisans, scholars, army officers, and experts in metallurgy, the Muscovite ambassadors always endeavored to recruit in Western Europe such persons of talent.

Ivan the Great might have asked the Greeks at his court to found schools, wherein new generations of Russians could be educated in modern progress. But such an idea did not occur to the ruler of the Kremlin. Consequently, the Renaissance never penetrated into the hearts of the Russian people, but merely cast a few reflected rays of its splendor on wintry Moscow.

Religious Unrest

The reign of Ivan III was disturbed by religious unrest. Two heretical sects arose in Novgorod and spread to Moscow. They were probably merely an echo of Western rationalist sectarianism. With the support of the Grand Princess Sophia, Joseph of Volokolamsk, a renowned churchman of the period, secured the death sentence for the heretical leaders (1504). It was the first time that heretics had been burned at the stake in Moscow.[5]

This same Joseph was a stanch defender of the growing wealth of the Russian monasteries. The monasteries founded in the wilderness had developed into huge agricultural estates cultivated by thousands of serfs, who labored in place of the monks. In 1503 Nilus Sorsky, one of the saintliest of Russia's ascetics, attacked the excessive wealth of the monasteries at a council held in Moscow. Joseph of Volokolamsk obstructed this daring attempt at reform, and the party of Joseph was victorious. Nilus Sorsky protested against the persecution of heretics. His letters to his followers are instinct with a fiery, vibrant charity.[6]

Complete Failure of Rome's Hopes

The marriage of Ivan the Great with Sophia Paleologus crystallized in the minds of the Russian masses the idea that Moscow was the third Rome, a city to which had been given a divinely appointed Orthodox mission. Even in a political sense Moscow appeared to the people as the successor of Constantinople. One of Sophia's brothers had gone to serve the Turks. The other tried to sell to various European sovereigns his hereditary titles to the Byzantine throne. Consequently, temporary opinion considered that these unworthy princes had forfeited their birthright.

Sophia was looked upon as the legitimate successor of the last Byzantine Emperor and by her marriage with Ivan she had transmitted to the ruler of Muscovy valid political rights to the throne of the Eastern Empire. Ivan the Great assumed the resounding title of Sovereign of All Russia, and took for the new arms of his realm the two-headed eagle of the Byzantine Emperors. The Russian ruler and people, dazzled by the consciousness of a splendid political and religious national destiny, were farther than ever from reunion with the Catholic Church.[7]

The third Basil (1505–1533), the son of Ivan the Great and the Byzantine Sophia, was the contemporary of Louis XI of France. He compares not unfavorably with that French ruler in creative cunning. Basil destroyed the liberties of Pskov, absorbed the last of the princely appanages, and won back from Lithuania the frontier town of Smolensk (1514). At the close of Basil's reign, the authority of Muscovy reached from Chernigov (77 miles above Kiev) northwestward to the Gulf of Finland, northward to the White Sea, and northeastward to the Ural Mountains. The Russian Empire was well on its expanding course.

Basil III exchanged embassies with all the sovereigns of Western Europe, except with those of France and of England. In the East the adventurous Baber, the Great Mogul of India, sought the Russian ruler's friendship.[8] At home Basil III increased the barbaric splendor of his court. This Muscovite ruler bore himself with such autocratic hauteur that the boyars looked back to Ivan the Great as having been more genial and accessible.

Basil III and His Clergy

Basil dealt in as highhanded a manner with his churchmen as with his boyars. For the time being, however, he was on friendly terms with the party of Joseph of Volokolamsk. In vain the monk Vassian, a pupil of Nilus Sorsky, attacked Joseph's followers. Joseph of Volokolamsk died (1515) in high favor with the Muscovite ruler, despite Vassian's eloquent indignation. The condition of the Russian Church had at that time palpably worsened. In the sixteenth century the Church held a third of all the landed property in Muscovy. The prelates did not dare to oppose the secular authority, for fear of losing their wealth.

Basil III discovered in the Kremlin library a great number of precious, but dust-covered, Greek manuscripts. He thereupon sent messengers to a famous monastery on Mount Athos in Greece and obtained the services of the monk Maxim to make new translations from Greek into Slavonic. Maxim had studied in Western Europe. Because he was an ardent admirer of the condemned Savonarola, he hated Rome. Maxim the Greek did much to increase in Russia dislike and distrust of Latin Christianity. He finally lost the favor of Basil III by criticizing the domestic life of the Russian ruler and was thrown into prison.

A man who was more fortunate in his friendship with Basil was the Western scholar, Nicholas Lue-Bulev, who served as personal physician to the Grand Prince. Basil permitted his Western friend to engage freely in public discussions on religious matters and to publish treatises urging reunion with the Holy See. Nicholas Lue-Bulev converted to Catholicism Theodore Karpov, one of the outstanding Muscovite diplomats of his time.[9]

Basil's general attitude toward Rome, however, was exactly the same as that of his father. He did not entertain the slightest notion of reunion with the Holy See, and he had no intention of enlisting in a European crusade against the Turks. But the wily Grand Prince greatly desired Western experts to aid him in the material development of his realm, and the Pope could facilitate the obtaining of such invaluable specialists. Accordingly, Basil instructed his envoys to give equivocal and evasive answers when questioned about religious matters.

Poland and the Pope's Envoys

Another reason for the Holy See's tragic contemporary ignorance of the true state of affairs in Muscovy was the attitude of Poland. That Catholic country did not wish her greatest enemy to benefit by friendship with Western Europe. In

1514 the victorious Sigismund I of Poland turned back at the frontier James Piso, a papal envoy to Moscow. But in 1518 the fortunes of war veered against Poland, and Sigismund was then willing to make use of papal negotiation with Basil III. Leo X sent northward the skilled Austrian diplomat, Baron Sigismund von Herberstein. A measure of success appears to have attended these negotiations, for the Pope then dispatched another envoy to Muscovy, Father Nicholas von Schönberg, a gifted Dominican priest. But at the moment King Sigismund felt that papal intervention in Moscow was not needed. So Father Nicholas von Schönberg never saw the Kremlin's crenelated walls.[10]

In 1519 Sigismund of Poland was once more imploring the good offices of the Holy See in securing peace terms from Muscovy. The long-suffering Leo X sent northward as envoys two Italian prelates, Zachary Ferreri and John Tedaldi. Meanwhile the Polish ruler had succeeded in patching up a truce with Basil III; thus he did not scruple to prevent the papal envoys from reaching the Russian capital.

Rome Baffled by Muscovy

In 1520 and again in 1523 an Italian adventurer by the name of Paul Centurione journeyed to Moscow. He was at first of the opinion that Muscovy could be won for Catholicism without much difficulty. On the occasion of Centurione's second journey Pope Clement VII (1523–1534) gave him a letter for the Grand Prince. Centurione returned from Muscovy in 1525, bringing with him a Russian ambassador, Demetrius Gerasimov. Great was the excitement in Rome over the arrival of Basil's envoy.

Gerasimov said that his master desired Clement VII to send an envoy to Moscow. The delighted Pope chose as his delegate Bishop John Francis Citus, a talented and zealous Franciscan. Basil III welcomed the Franciscan prelate, consented to a truce with Poland and Sweden, and asked in return that the Pope aid him to recruit experts in Western Europe. But on May 5, 1527, the mercenaries of Emperor Charles V sacked Rome. The Holy Father, in exile at Orvieto, could do little toward assembling the Western experts requested by Basil III.[11]

In 1528 Basil sent to Rome another envoy, by the name of Trusov. The Grand Prince spoke of joining in the war against the Turks. Clement VII never perceived the truth about Muscovy and the character of its cunning ruler. A sovereign of such small personal courage as Basil III could never have been counted upon as an ally against the Turks. And Sophia's son was so little inclined to recognize the universal jurisdiction of the Holy See that he addressed the Pope as merely "a doctor of the Roman Church."

Basil Cuts Off His Beard

Salome, the first wife of Basil III, had been chosen according to old custom from among fifteen hundred of the most noble and comely maidens in the whole realm. But during twenty-one years the beautiful Salome had borne Basil no child. The aging Grand Prince at length divorced his barren consort. He had fallen in love with Helen Glinsky, a handsome and vivacious young Ukrainian from Lithuania. The Muscovites were shocked by Basil's divorce from his lawful wife, but the Grand Prince himself was so fascinated by his young bride that he even cut off his beard to please her. This was a further scandal to his subjects, because the Orthodox Church condemned the shaving of beards as an indication of culpable effeminacy.

Basil III lived only long enough after this second marriage for Helen to bear him two sons. The younger of those sons was feeble-minded; the elder would reign as Ivan the Terrible. The impetuous widow of the Grand Prince alienated everyone by her haughty ways and by an imprudent love affair with her master of the horse. She died five years after Basil III, apparently of poison.[12]

At the time when the young mother of Ivan the Terrible thus met a violent end, the Holy See had not achieved the slightest contact with the immense majority of the Russian people. Those toiling peasant masses were then traveling farther and farther along the dreary road to outright serfdom.

Footnotes to Chapter Three

1 V. O. Klyuchevsky, *A History of Russia.* Vol. II, p. 490.
2 Paul Pierling, *La Russie et le Saint-Siège.* Vol. I, pp. 136–73.
3 Alfred Rambaud, *A Popular History of Russia.* Vol. I, p. 231.
4 Paul Pierling, *op. cit.,* Vol. I, p. 248.
5 J. N. Danzas, *The Russian Church,* pp. 21–24.
6 G. P. Fedotov, editor, *A Treasury of Russian Spirituality,* pp. 85–133.
7 Nicolas Zernov, *The Russians and Their Church,* pp. 50–53.
8 Alexandre Eck, *Le Moyen Age Russe,* p. 438.
9 Paul Pierling, *op. cit.* Vol. I, p. 286.
10 Ludwig von Pastor, *The History of the Popes.* Vol. VII, p. 238.
11 Ludwig von Pastor, *op. cit.* Vol. X, pp. 366 f.
12 S. F. Platonov, *A History of Russia,* p. 125.

CHAPTER FOUR

The Czar and the Jesuit

AFTER THE sudden death of his Lithuanian mother, the eight-year-old Ivan IV (1533–1584) and Yury, his feeble-minded brother, were kept alive in a semblance of power only because two princely families were then vying furiously with each other for the regency. It was a time of outright anarchy. The royal orphans were ill-clothed and often even cold and hungry. Only when foreign ambassadors arrived did the boyars dress Ivan in cloth of gold and fall on their faces before him.

The moody, lonely, and brilliant Ivan brooded over the injuries done to him and read avidly about powerful autocrats of the past. At the age of thirteen, he suddenly asserted himself, meting out cruel punishments to great boyars who had neglected and abused him. Four years later, in 1547, Ivan placed the crown on his own head in a splendid ceremony and he announced that his title would be, not Grand Prince, but Czar and Autocrat of All Russia. At the time of his self-coronation Ivan chose as bride Anastasia Romanov, of a boyar family which was deservedly popular among the poorer classes. The gentle Anastasia had a happy influence on her strange young husband.

Two months after Ivan's coronation a great fire broke out in Moscow. Almost two thousand victims perished in the holocaust of the city's wooden dwellings. The populace, egged on by hostile boyars, claimed that the ruler's Glinsky relatives had caused the disaster. A riot took place during which a Glinsky prince was murdered. Ivan himself accepted the catastrophe as a warning of divine displeasure. He resolved henceforth to reign worthily and so to win the support of his people as a whole. Then he would be able to deal as he wished with the arrogant, great boyars. The young sovereign accordingly picked advisers to whom he gave the name of the Chosen Council, and agreed to do nothing without their approval. The following six years were to be the happiest of his otherwise nightmarish reign.

New Mystifications

In that same year of 1547 there was at Ivan's court a certain unscrupulous German adventurer, by the name of Hans Schlitte. The Czar had not lost sight of his hereditary enemies on the western frontier, so he sent Schlitte to recruit men of war and armorers in Western Europe. In 1550 Schlitte brazenly deceived an esteemed Austrian nobleman, by the name of John Steinberg. Schlitte's story was to the effect that the Czar had empowered him to appoint for Muscovy a "Latin and German chancellor." His choice had therefore fallen on Steinberg, and he urged the latter to go at once to Rome to negotiate with the Holy See the conditions of Russia's return to the Catholic fold.

With more zeal than worldly wisdom the good Steinberg proceeded to undertake the affairs of Muscovy. He was cordially welcomed in Rome by Pope Julius III (1551). It was the age of the Catholic Restoration, when the Council of Trent and the Jesuits were powerfully rekindling missionary ardor. A special body of cardinals was appointed to deal with Steinberg's supposed mission, and the following year the Holy See informed Sigismund-Augustus II of Poland that there was hope for the reunion of Russia and Rome.

The Polish ruler forthwith set to work to move heaven and earth to persuade the Pope not to enter into relations with Moscow. At that time Poland was riddled with heresy. Julius III could not afford to alienate a Catholic ruler in favor of a vague project of reunion with Muscovy. The poor Steinberg was granted no further hearing in Rome. In 1553 the Pope assured Sigismund-Augustus that the Holy See would not establish relations with Ivan without having previously notified the Polish sovereign.[1]

Champion of the People

As for Ivan IV, it appears that he was never aware of the vast hoax perpetrated in his name by Hans Schlitte. In those years he had been ruling his people wisely and winning military successes. In 1550 the young Czar called together an assembly of the nation (*Zemsky Sobor*) intended to represent all classes. In eloquent words Ivan promised this gathering that henceforth he himself would be the defender of "the people of God and given me by God." The enthusiastic populace began to look on the fiery young ruler as their special champion.

In 1552 Ivan led a large army against the Tartar stronghold of Kazan, situated almost at the junction of the Volga and the Kama, a mighty tributary affording access to the Urals. Kazan fell after a bitterly contested struggle. In 1553 a Tartar prince favorable to Muscovy was chosen at Astrakhan, at the mouth of the Volga; this Tartar metropolis was later annexed without difficulty. It was in Ivan's time that the old State of Muscovy burst its bounds and expanded into the structure of a Russian nation.

Shortly after the fall of Kazan a daring English explorer, Captain Chancellor, reached Moscow by way of the White Sea and the eastern Dvina River. Chancellor was received by Ivan with marked favor, and in 1555 the Englishman returned to Moscow as the ambassador of Queen Mary. The Czar granted great privileges to English merchants. He wished to develop his one sure outlet to the West, and to obtain from England military and technical experts to aid him in his struggle against Continental enemies.[2]

Ivan came near to death in 1553, and he desired that his Council of Boyars should swear allegiance to his wife and his infant son. As the Czar lay on his sickbed, he heard the boyars in the adjoining room voicing their opposition to his wife's family. Ivan recovered, but he brooded somberly over the desertion of the boyars and planned the traitors' destruction.

Ivan IV was eager to secure for Russia an outlet to the Baltic Sea. With this end in view he moved against the moribund Knights of the Sword in Livonia in 1558. The Knights of the Sword broke under the assault, but they ceded Livonia to Poland. Ivan thereupon took the town of Polotsk from Poland. Then the Poles, in their turn, won a victory. But Sigismund-Augustus asked for peace and was willing to cede all that the Czar had conquered.

The Tenacious Pius IV

Meanwhile, the sessions of the Council of Trent, already twice interrupted, were about to be resumed. According to previous custom all European rulers, dissident as well as Catholic, should be summoned to a general council. Pius IV therefore attempted to notify the Russian Czar. As usual, Poland opposed the passage of the Pope's messengers. The second papal envoy, John Giraldi, was actually thrown into a Polish jail. By the time that Giraldi had been released, the final session of the Council of Trent (1563) had already been held.

Though Rome was ignorant of the fact, a sinister change for the worse had at that time darkened the soul of Ivan IV. His beloved Anastasia had died, and the Czar was obsessed by the conviction that traitorous boyars had poisoned his wife. In 1561 Ivan the Terrible carried out the first mass execution of his enemies, real or supposed. After Anastasia's death Ivan married again almost at once, choosing as his second wife a Circassian girl of fierce instincts. The Czar survived this second bride, and when he died he had had in all seven wives, several of whom were of Tartar strain.

Pius IV was tenacious in the performance of his apostolic duties. If he had not been able to invite Ivan to the council, he would at least acquaint Russia with the decrees that had been promulgated at Trent. In 1565 the Holy Father made arrangements to send a zealous Franciscan missioner to Moscow, but for some reason this project never reached the stage of definite action.[3]

The Terror

In 1564 Ivan began a frightful reign of terror. The Czar had evolved a mad but deadly scheme for the destruction of the great boyars. At the same time he assured the people as a whole that he was their friend and only sought to safeguard them from their oppressors. Ivan left the government of the nation nominally to the boyars, but he reserved to himself all the real resources of power.

The despot set aside for himself a special domain, in which he was surrounded by his own army and black-garbed secret police. The boyars denounced by the secret police were given no opportunity to defend themselves; they were immediately tortured and slain. Often their whole family perished with them. When Ivan could not sleep well at night, he soothed his nerves by descending a private stairway to watch the tortures of would-be fugitives who had been captured on their way to Lithuania.

In 1570 the Czar suspected the Novgorodians of negotiations with Poland. He marched on the city and carried on during five weeks a ghastly slaughter of the inhabitants. Whole families were thrown into the river, and police in boats pushed them under the ice. The Volkhov was choked with corpses.

Metropolitan Philip did not hesitate to rebuke Ivan for his cruelties, and the courageous churchman paid for his integrity with his life. In general, Ivan's attitude toward the Russian Church was arrogantly highhanded. The Czar assumed the title of "Father of the Church and State," and a synod obediently approved the despot's claim of being the highest authority in ecclesiastical affairs.[4]

Embittered Russian boyars had a traitorous revenge on Ivan in 1571. They guided Crimean Tartars through the military cordon that protected Moscow. The Tartars burned most of the city and carried off southward 130,000 Muscovites to be sold as slaves. In 1572 the Czar suddenly abolished his own separatist government. Ivan had managed to cripple the boyar class so that it never recovered its former strength, but he did not succeed in creating a substitute for the old government. The visionary Czar destroyed more than he created.

Ivan Turns to the Pope

Pope Gregory XIII was deeply zealous for the propagation of the Faith. In 1576 he founded on the banks of the Tiber the College of St. Athanasius for Greek and Slav students. The papal nuncio in Poland was instructed to recruit students for this college in the Russian provinces of Poland, and to secure a Muscovite student, perhaps a prisoner of war. Before many years had passed the College of St. Athanasius was rendering great service to the cause of reunion by training able Slav apostles.[5]

Meantime, King Sigismund-Augustus of Poland had been succeeded by Stephen Bathory of Transylvania, a man of notable military ability. Under the vigorous leadership of Bathory the disciplined troops of Poland were winning victories over Ivan's ill-equipped soldiery. At length Bathory had Ivan so badly cornered that the astute Czar determined to ask the Pope to act as mediator. Ivan sent three envoys to Rome in 1581.

Pope Gregory XIII chose as his delegate to Moscow Father Antonio Possevino, a brilliant Italian Jesuit who had successfully combatted Protestantism in France, Poland, and Sweden.[6] Father Possevino journeyed to Staritza on the Volga, where Ivan was temporarily residing, and presented the Pope's letter and gifts to the Czar. Gregory XIII skillfully urged in his letter that religious union was the only feasible basis for political union in a European league against the Turks.[7] Possevino then proceeded to a frontier village. There, living in a primitive hut in the depth of winter, the courageous Jesuit negotiated the terms of a ten years' truce between Russia and Poland.

From the frontier village the Pope's envoy went to Moscow, where he was received by Ivan in the Kremlin. Now that peace with Poland had been obtained, the Czar was evasive in regard to the anti-Turkish league, and he would not consent to the building of a Catholic church in Muscovy. Ivan was proud of his theological learning, so he engaged in personal debate with the Jesuit.

The Czar maintained that certain Popes had proved themselves unworthy of the primacy. The Jesuit replied that it was with the Popes as with the Czars: there were good and bad of both, but their rights and prerogatives were always the same, no matter who filled the office. Ivan cried out that the Pope was not a shepherd, but a wolf. Possevino replied calmly that it was a wonder the Czar had sought the mediation of a wolf. Then Ivan the Terrible gave a loud cry and lifted his iron-tipped staff to strike at the Catholic priest. The bystanders cringed in horror, but Possevino did not flinch and the Czar regained control of his rage.

When the Jesuit returned to Rome, he was accompanied by Iakov Molvianinov, the Czar's envoy. The Holy See negotiated with the boorish ambassador without result. In the autumn of 1582 Possevino returned northward in the company of Molvianinov. At Warsaw the travelers parted. Possevino remained at Bathory's court, while the Russian continued on to Moscow. That brought to an end the relations between Ivan IV and the Holy See.[8]

Somber Last Years

The closing period of Ivan's reign was somber. In a fit of anger he had killed his own eldest son and heir. Feodor, the elder of the Czar's remaining sons, was feeble-minded; and Dmitry, Ivan's son by his seventh wife, was a mere infant. Much of Moscow still lay in the ruins caused by the invasion of the Crimean Tartars. At the conclusion of his northern war Ivan had been obliged to cede all his gains to Poland and Sweden. Thousands of peasants had fled the crushing authority of Moscow, so that entire villages in central Russia had emptied overnight. The runaway peasants drifted to those frontier regions where the Cossacks, the "masterless men," dwelt in democratic brotherhoods.

The one bright flash of joy in the desolation of Ivan's last years was the work of migrant Cossack adventurers. Led by Ermak, a Don Cossack who was under sentence of death, a band of these freebooters crossed the Urals and seized Sibir, the stronghold of the Siberian ruler, Kuchum. Ermak handed over his conquest to the Czar, in return for a full pardon. The Russian march to the Pacific had begun.[9]

Ivan the Terrible died in one of his sudden fits of passion on March 27, 1584. At the passing of this unhappy and sinister ruler Rome was as far as ever from establishing fruitful contact with Russia. Father Possevino's arguments in favor of reunion had served merely to infuriate the terrible Czar. Moreover, during the Jesuit's stay in Moscow, he had been so closely watched over by a "guard of honor" that he had not been able to talk with any member of the Russian masses.[10]

Footnotes to Chapter Four

[1] Ludwig von Pastor, *History of the Popes.* Vol. XIII, p. 236.
[2] K. Waliszewski, *Ivan the Terrible,* pp. 273–78.
[3] Paul Pierling, *La Russie et le Saint-Siège.* Vol. I, pp. 369–74.
[4] Joseph B. Koncevicius, *Russia's Attitude Towards Union With Rome,* pp. 91–93.
[5] Paul Pierling, *op. cit.* Vol. I, pp. 403 f.
[6] Martin Harney, *The Jesuits in History,* pp. 129, 133 f., 140–43, 181.
[7] Antonio Possevino, *Moscovia et Alia Opera,* p. 58.
[8] Paul Pierling, *op. cit.* Vol. II, pp. 97–208.
[9] Harold Lamb, *The March of Muscovy,* pp. 199–206.
[10] Ludwig von Pastor, *op. cit.* Vol. XX, p. 444.

CHAPTER FIVE

Catholics in the Kremlin

IF CZAR FEODOR (1584–1598) was weak in body and simple in mind, he was sound in his religious faith and moral judgment. He put an end to bloodshed and to cruel oppression. The Muscovites loved Feodor. They considered him as one of those "fools in Christ" whom they believed to be under God's special protection.[1]

Czar Feodor left all the affairs of government in the capable hands of his brother-in-law, Boris Godunov, a gifted boyar of Tartar origin, who had served as one of the chief agents of Ivan IV in the despot's later years. Boris Godunov proved himself a great regent by restoring to Russia prosperity and prestige. The conquest of Siberia continued, and in the southeast Muscovy had already reached the Caucasus.

During the past few decades a steady stream of Ukrainians in Lithuania and Poland had been returning to their former home and recolonizing the lower Dnieper. Fugitive peasants from Muscovy were taking the same direction. The more determined seekers of liberty among the peasant settlers joined the free brotherhood of Cossacks in the Zaporog fastness, on islands below the rapids of the Dnieper River. From 1600 onward the Zaporog Cossacks were feared on every coast of the Black Sea.

Meanwhile, Stephen Bathory had been dreaming of a great Slav State, supreme in the East. The Polish ruler planned to annex Muscovy, and then to march against the Turks. Bathory sought the financial aid of Pope Sixtus V (1585–1590) for the realization of these grandiose projects, but all his plans came to nought. He died childless in 1586. The Polish nobles chose as Bathory's successor the Catholic Prince Sigismund of Sweden. Two years later Sigismund's father died, and the disputed succession to the Swedish throne led to a northern war in which Russia recovered some of the territory lost to Sweden under Ivan IV.[2]

Appointment of a Russian Patriarch

Ever since the Turks had won Constantinople the Russian prelates had been loath to recognize the authority of a Patriarch subject to the infidel sultan. Boris arranged for Jeremias II, Patriarch of Constantinople, to visit Moscow. In 1589 Jeremias was persuaded to consecrate a special Patriarch of Moscow and All-Russia. From this time onward the Russian Church became increasingly dependent on the secular power.

In 1591 the ten-year-old Prince Dmitry, half brother of Czar Feodor, died under mysterious circumstances in his appanage of Uglich. Later, when Feodor died, the political rivals of Boris Godunov would accuse him of having contrived the murder of Prince Dmitry, the rightful heir to the throne.

Pope Clement VIII (1592–1605) strove to form a great coalition against the Turks. Alexander Komulovic, rector of the Yugoslav Church of San Girolamo in Rome, was ordered to interest Czar Feodor in the war against the infidels. Komulovic went to Feodor's court in 1595 and again in 1597, but his zealous efforts in Russia proved fruitless. The Muscovites had heard that the Catholic Slavic priest had encouraged the Ukrainians in Poland-Lithuania to unite with the Holy See.[3]

Boris Godunov found a way to please the lesser gentry in 1597. The lands of the lesser nobility ran the risk of being depopulated for the benefit of the great boyars, who did everything to attract the peasants to their estates. Boris forbade the peasants to pass from one estate to another, thus taking the fatal initial step of tying the Russian peasants to the soil. His temporary measures afterwards became permanent laws, reducing the peasants to outright serfdom.

The Union of Brest-Litovsk

During several decades the Jesuits in Poland-Lithuania had been laboring to reunite the Ukrainians or Ruthenians (Little Russians) to the Holy See. Active apostles of reunion were the renowned Father Peter Skarga and the ubiquitous Father Antonio Possevino. At this time the condition of the Ruthenian Church was deplorable. The Ruthenian Orthodox clergy had fallen into ignorance and lacked moral vigor. Meanwhile, lay religious confraternities interfered in ecclesiastical matters.

In 1589 Patriarch Jeremias of Constantinople, on his return from Moscow, remained for some time among the Ruthenians. He authorized the religious lay confraternities of Lemberg and Vilna to watch over the orthodoxy of their pastors and even of their bishops. As a result a number of the Ruthenian prelates began to entertain the idea of reuniting with Rome. King Sigismund III was eager for the reunion, because he realized the dangerous attraction of the new Patriarch of Moscow for his Ruthenian subjects.

The Metropolitan of Kiev, Michael Rahoza, called together several Ruthenian bishops at Brest-Litovsk in 1595. They drew up a joint letter to Pope Clement VIII proposing reunion, provided that they might preserve their Byzantine liturgy and ritual. In Rome the Pope awaited with joyous expectation the delegates of the Ruthenian hierarchy. He hoped that a Uniate Church in Poland might serve as a natural bridge to elusive Muscovy. On December 23, 1595, the reunion of the Ruthenians with the Holy See was proclaimed in a splendid ceremony at the Vatican.[4]

Unfortunately, Metropolitan Rahoza did not convoke a council for the solemn proclamation in Poland of the union until October, 1596. Meanwhile the supporters of schism raised a powerful agitation against the union. Finally the party of schism won over the majority of the Ruthenian aristocracy and people, who withdrew their allegiance from the Uniate bishops. In spite of all opposition there were soon over twelve million Ukrainian Catholics, but persecution came speedily and was to last for centuries. The Union of Brest-Litovsk vastly inflamed Muscovite hatred of the Catholic Church.[5]

"Not a Born Czar"

In 1598 the ancient dynasty of Rurik flickered out with the death of the feeble Feodor. Boris Godunov, who had filled the State with his own officials, succeeded to the deceased sovereign. Czar Boris formed a bodyguard of German troops from the Baltic, and he enlisted the services of Western architects and artisans. He had his sons taught by foreigners, and he sent Russian youths to study abroad. This Tartar on the throne of the Czars stood out as the first "Westernizer" in the line of Russian sovereigns.

In spite of the prosperity of the opening years of the reign of Boris Godunov, it was felt that this Tartar ruler was "not a born Czar," and he himself lived in a constant state of fear and suspicion. In 1601 he had the Romanov relatives of Czar Feodor deported. Feodor Romanov, the eldest, was forced to become a monk, under the name of Philaret, and his wife was sent to a convent. Both parents were thus separated from their little son, Michael.

From 1601 to 1604 there was a great famine in Russia, which the populace viewed as God's punishment for the murder of Prince Dmitry. The people even murmured against the charity of Czar Boris, saying that he dispensed "the blood of the innocent in a golden vase." [6] Then appeared a pretender, who said that he was the real Dmitry and that another child had been buried at Uglich in his stead.

The False Dmitry

This young man was probably a Russian gentleman who had fled to Lithuania to escape punishment for a serious crime. He persuaded a Polish magnate, a certain Mniszek, that he, not Boris, was the rightful Czar. The adventurer also fell in love with the magnate's daughter, Marina. The mysterious pretender was received into the Catholic Church by a Jesuit in April, 1604, and the convert expressed great zeal for the cause of reuniting Russia to Rome.

King Sigismund of Poland dared not break openly with Czar Boris, but in secret he encouraged his nobles to take up "Dmitry's" cause. In this extremity Boris Godunov even tried to obtain the mediation of the Pope against the impostor, but the Muscovite ruler's letter arrived in Rome at a time when the Holy See was vacant. Accompanied by numerous Poles and Russian exiles, the pretender invaded Muscovy. He was soon joined by forty thousand Cossacks. On April 13, 1605, Czar Boris suddenly died. "Dmitry" entered the capital in triumph and was gladly accepted as Czar by the populace of Moscow.

Czar Dmitry restored the Romanovs to favor. Feodor Romanov, now the monk Philaret, was appointed Metropolitan of Rostov. The new sovereign made Patriarch an obsequious Greek prelate by the name of Ignatius, who was an avowed enemy of Catholicism. In spite of this the two Polish Jesuits who had accompanied Dmitry's army of invasion as chaplains did not lose faith in the illustrious convert. They believed the Czar's assurances that it was absolutely necessary for him to give an appearance of stanch Orthodoxy at the start.[7]

The Catholic Czar's Brief Rule

Czar Dmitry sent one of his Jesuit chaplains to discuss with Pope Paul V (1605–1621) the project of a coalition against the Turks. The Pope dispatched northward Father Alexander Rangoni, who received a gracious welcome at Czar Dmitry's court. The Czar told Rangoni that he was planning to send a solemn embassy to Rome, and in the Eternal City hopes of reunion were high.

Meanwhile the boyars at Czar Dmitry's court noted with anger and suspicion that the young ruler flouted ancient national customs. The Poles, too, were disappointed in their protégé. Now that the adventurer was safely installed on the throne, he would not cede any Russian territory to Sigismund III. In secret some of the boyars offered the crown to Sigismund's son. The final catastrophe was hastened by the costly festivities attending the arrival in Moscow and the coronation of the beautiful, gay Marina Mniszek. The Czar's bride was accompanied by numerous Polish gentry who treated the Muscovites with arrogant disdain, while the rascally servants of these Poles robbed and raped as if they were in conquered territory.

On May 27, 1606, a scheming princely boyar, Basil Shuisky, led an armed attack on the Kremlin. Czar Dmitry jumped or was thrown from a window. His body was exposed on the Red Square. Then the remains of the false Dmitry were burned, and his ashes were fired from a cannon in the direction of Poland whence he came. The reign of the Catholic Czar had lasted only eleven months.[8]

Confusion Confounded

Basil Shuisky organized a mob on the Red Square, who obediently demanded his election as Czar. But Shuisky had no control over the boyars. A new false Dmitry arose, supported by Polish adventurers and by Cossacks from the Dnieper and the Don. This brutal man camped close outside Moscow, and seized more and more towns. Russia was demoralized. Then King Sigismund of Poland entered the picture, obtaining the blessing of Pope Paul V for the conquest of Muscovy by a Catholic sovereign.

The Poles defeated Czar Basil Shuisky's army in the summer of 1610. Shuisky died in a Polish prison. In their fear of the pretender the boyars invited the Poles to enter Moscow. The invaders imprisoned the heroic Patriarch Hermogen, slaughtered thousands of the citizens, and burned most of Moscow, with the exception of the Kremlin. In December, 1610, the second false Dmitry was killed by one of his Tartar followers. His death brought a sharp turn in Russian sentiment. The people ceased to place their hopes in this or that impersonator of a "born sovereign," and all classes began to feel the need of an agreement to drive out the hated Poles.

The People Save Russia

In 1611 a popular uprising for the national deliverance was organized by Cosmo Minin, a butcher of Nizhny-Novgorod, and the patriotic Prince Dmitry Pozharsky. Other towns of northern and northeastern Russia joined the uprising and Prince Pozharsky led his growing army toward Moscow. In the capital the Poles starved Patriarch Hermogen to death, after the aged prelate had refused to dissuade his subjects from resistance. The followers of Minin and Pozharsky then had the memory of a martyr as their inspiration.[9]

With the aid of the Cossacks Pozharsky's troops stormed

Moscow and on November 27, 1612, the Poles in the Kremlin surrendered. The nation would still be disordered for many years to come, but the crisis of the Time of Troubles had safely passed. After the deliverance of the capital a national assembly was called, with representatives from all the Russian towns and from all classes. On February 21, 1613, the national assembly unanimously elected Czar the young Michael Romanov, who was connected by marriage with Ivan the Terrible, of the ancient dynasty of Rurik.

Poland had lost her great opportunity of uniting the Slavonic world. Until the Time of Troubles the ordinary people in Muscovy had not come into contact with Catholics. Then they encountered Catholic Poles as detested invaders of the Fatherland, and their hatred for the Catholic Church was thenceforth nourished by intense personal bitterness. Was not the Pope himself an ally of treacherous Poland? Could the Russian masses ever forget how the Catholic invaders had slaughtered in cold blood thousands of Muscovites, and had starved their saintly Patriarch to death because he loved his country? [10]

Footnotes to Chapter Five

[1] Nicolas Zernov, *The Russians and Their Church,* pp. 67–69.
[2] Paul Pierling, *La Russie et le Saint-Siège.* Vol. II, pp. 240–317.
[3] *Ibid.,* pp. 330–68.
[4] Cesare S. Baronius, *Annales ecclesiastici.* Tome VII, pp. 859 ff.
[5] Ludwig von Pastor, *History of the Popes.* Vol. XXIV, pp. 125–40.
[6] S. F. Platonov, *Boris Godounov, Tsar de Russie,* pp. 247–50.
[7] Paul Pierling, *op. cit.* Vol. III, pp. 47–118.
[8] *Ibid.,* pp. 118–340.
[9] S. F. Platonov, *A History of Russia,* pp. 159–70.
[10] Helen Iswolsky, *Soul of Russia,* p. 30.

CHAPTER SIX

Rome Remembers

AFTER THE Time of Troubles, the gory ghost of the false Dmitry rose up between the Kremlin and the Vatican. Russia had no desire to renew official relations with Rome, so long as there existed no urgent political motive for an understanding. Rome was less forgetful. The Turks continued to press on Christendom, and the Holy See longed to enlist Russia in the struggle against Islam.

During the reigns of Czar Michael (1613–1645) and Czar Alexis (1645–1676), the Russian Uniates were exposed to pressure and persecution. Because many of the Ruthenian nobles and large landowners were yielding to Polish influences and passing to the Latin rite, Pope Urban VIII in 1624 forbade the Ruthenians to pass from the Byzantine to the Latin rite without the special permission of the Holy See.[1]

At this period, hatred of Catholicism was especially bitter among Russians in lands which had been ceded to Poland in the peace treaty after the Time of Troubles. The saintly Uniate prelate of Polotsk, Bishop Josaphat Kuncevich, was attacked by an Orthodox mob in 1623, stabbed, and thrown into the Dvina River. The martyr was canonized in Rome in 1867. The terrible Polish reprisals against Saint Josaphat's murderers served to widen the chasm separating Russia from the Catholic Church.

In 1620 an Orthodox hierarchy was set up in the Ukraine, and the attacks of the Dnieper Cossacks forced the Polish ruler to recognize the Orthodox prelates. The ancient city of Kiev was lost to the Union in 1633, and the famous Orthodox theologian, Peter Moghila, became its spiritual head. The Uniate Metropolitan continued to have the title of Kiev, but resided henceforth at Radomysl.

After the erection of the Orthodox hierarchy in Little Russia, the Uniates were harassed by Cossacks, Lutheran Swedes, and Tartars. When Kiev passed to Russia through an alliance with the Dnieper Cossacks, the Uniate problem became even more acute. In 1653 Czar Alexis sent envoys to request Poland to suppress the Union, but King John Casimir held firm. The position of the Uniates improved after the election of the vigorous John Sobieski to the throne of Poland (1674).

Peter Moghila

Metropolitan Peter Moghila, a monk of the Kiev Monastery of the Caves, had studied philosophy and theology in Paris. In an effort to raise the standard of Orthodox education this remarkable man founded the Kiev Orthodox Academy. Instruction at the Kiev Academy was given principally in Latin, the *Summa Theologica* of Saint Thomas was expounded, and the whole course of studies was modeled on that of the Jesuit colleges. The best students of the Academy were sent to Rome to complete their studies. Peter Moghila also wrote a catechism approved by the Greek Church and by Patriarch Adrian of Moscow. In general, the doctrine of Peter Moghila's catechism is Catholic.[2]

A branch of the Kiev Academy was founded in Moscow. But for the most part, Russian monks were not scholars; they had been taught to consider science and rhetoric as manifestations of worldliness. Consequently, the cultured monks of the Kiev Academy were regarded with suspicion by their less learned Muscovite confreres, and they were thus unable to exercise any considerable influence on the Russian Church.

Seventeenth-Century Developments

Klyuchevsky says of the slow and painful expansion of Russia's frontiers during the seventeenth century that "the State swelled and the people grew thin." The national assembly, which had elected Michael Romanov, gradually dwindled to nothing. Laws were passed attaching the peasants more and more irrevocably to the soil.

Western influence increased. Foreign military instructors were secured to train the Russian troops in European tactics. The Russian Government employed Western experts to investigate the mineral wealth of the nation. The harbor of Archangel was improved. At this period, Muscovy served as a means of commercial communication between Europe and Asia, and at Moscow a special suburb was set aside for the foreigners. Under the influence of foreign relations, commercial capitalism developed and spread to internal trade.[3]

Metropolitan Philaret, the father of Czar Michael Romanov, was made Patriarch. During the best years of Czar Michael's reign his father was associated with the throne. Czar and Patriarch figured together in all public acts, and together received the reports of boyars and foreign ambassadors.

Russian adventurers continued their advance across thinly populated Siberia. Peasant cultivators, the true colonists, followed the daring Siberian pioneers. Small wooden churches, and then monasteries, appeared in the more populous settlements. When Czar Michael died in 1645, his capital contained

40,000 homes and was one of the largest cities in Europe. But most of Moscow's houses were wooden, and disastrous fires were of frequent occurrence.

The "Most Quiet" Czar

Alexis Romanov (1645–1676) was beloved of his people, who called him "most quiet and peaceful." Soon after his accession, the young Alexis had to face serious riots, caused by the bad government of his late father's favorites. Under the influence of these alarming uprisings, Czar Alexis issued a new code of law (1649) which made serfdom a State institution. It was an irony of history that the gentle Alexis was driven by the disordered times to confirm the establishment of serfdom.

A disastrous crisis in the life of the Russian Church occurred during this reign. A much-needed revision of the Muscovite Church books was put through with remarkable vigor by Patriarch Nikon, a keenly intelligent, but too intransigent man. Czar Alexis loved Nikon and granted him great power, but he could not persuade the Patriarch to soften his harsh ways. It was unfortunate that a man of Nikon's character should have taken up the delicate task of correcting Church books in a country where numerous champions of the "pure religion" were ready to lay down their lives to prevent the smallest changes.

Nikon's only reply to his opponents was to punish them, and thus took place in the Russian Church the grievous schism of the Old Believers. The numbers of the schismatics soon mounted into the thousands. Many gifted priests and whole monasteries refused to accept Nikon's reforms. The ranks of the Patriarch's enemies increased. In 1658 he lost the friendship of Alexis, resigned his office, and withdrew to a monastery. The corrected books were retained, but in 1666 Nikon was finally deposed.

Nikon left a profoundly shaken Church, which had lost its

hold over large groups of the people. The Oriental Patriarchs who had assembled in Moscow to condemn Nikon also excommunicated the Old Believers, many thousands of whom perished on the gallows or at the stake. Persecution merely swelled the ranks of the schismatics. Inevitably they broke up into various sects, some of which were weirdly fanatical.[4]

Among the Old Believers was the violent, warmly tender, and gifted Archpriest Avvakum, who endured years of cruel exile in Siberia. After his return to Moscow Avvakum remained obdurate. He was sent to a prison in the extreme northeast of European Russia. There the Archpriest wrote his wonderful autobiography, without question the masterpiece of Muscovite literature. In 1682 Avvakum was burned at the stake. "Satan has obtained our radiant Russia from God, so that she may become crimson with the blood of martyrs. Well planned, devil! It pleases us, too, to suffer for our dear Christ's sake," said the indomitably heroic Old Believer.[5]

In 1667 a Cossack of the Don River, Stenka Razin, led a great rebellion in southeastern Russia. His followers killed serf owners, plundered churches, looted ships, and introduced mob rule. Stenka Razin was finally defeated by the Czar's troops in 1671. Disorders continued and were put down only by pitched battles. One hundred thousand persons perished in the repression.

The Impact of Western Europe

At this period the turbulent gentry of Poland had weakened their nation by fantastic disorders. Sweden and Turkey were then much more dangerous to Muscovy than Poland, so in 1667 the able Russian statesman, Ordyn-Naschokin, concluded peace with Poland. It became the policy of Russia to support Poland against Turkey and Sweden, the common enemies.

Ordyn-Naschokin did not fear to borrow from the West. "There is no shame in borrowing what is good, even from your enemies," he said. This enlightened minister held that it was not enough for the Government to be always taking from its subjects; the State must also aid its peasants and its traders to produce riches. The majordomo of Czar Alexis, Feodor Rtistchev, was learned and open-minded. He founded in Moscow a school of theology, philosophy, and rhetoric, directed by monks from the Kiev Academy.

Alexis chose Simeon Polotsky, a brilliant monk of the Kiev Academy, as tutor of Feodor, the Czar's son by his first wife, Maria Miloslavsky. Sophia, the clever sister of Feodor, shared the benefits of Simeon's teaching.

The second wife of Czar Alexis, Natalia Naryshkin, was the ward of Matveyev, a friend and counselor of the sovereign, who knew Latin and Greek and kept open house for a circle of enlightened friends. The gay and attractive Natalia came of an obscure family with Tartar blood in its ancestry. Czarevitch Feodor was sickly and his brother, Ivan, was a stuttering idiot. There were six Miloslavsky princesses. The children of Maria Miloslavsky could not but be uneasy when their young stepmother gave birth to a healthy boy, who was christened Peter.

Elusive Muscovy

In 1672 the Turks attacked Poland, and Czar Alexis made ready to defend his ally against the invaders. Alexis sent an envoy to Rome, because it was believed that the Pope would exercise a strong influence in urging the secular rulers of Western Europe to join in the struggle against Islam. The Czar chose for the mission to Rome Paul Menzies, a Catholic Scotchman then in Moscow. At that time the aged Clement X sat on the throne of Peter; hence the diplomatic relations of the Holy See were carried on by Clement's nephew, Cardinal Pauluzzi, who had little knowledge of world affairs.

The Czar's Scottish ambassador made an excellent impression in Rome, and all went well until it was a question of the Russian ruler's titles. Moscow had stipulated that the Pope should address Alexis as Czar, otherwise Clement's brief would not be accepted at the Kremlin. The Pope's nephew refused to make the desired concession. Menzies was therefore obliged to refuse the papal brief, in which his employer was not addressed as Czar.

Pope Innocent XI (1676–1689) was anxious to make the concession refused to Menzies by the nephew of his predecessor. Poland and Russia were about to form an alliance against Turkey, and the Holy Father planned to send an envoy to Moscow in the company of the Polish ambassadors. But these plans were frustrated by a temporary break between Russia and Poland.

Rome had not succeeded in drawing any closer to Russia. When Alexis died in January, 1676, on a day when a white mantle of snow muffled the Kremlin, the gentle Czar believed as firmly as any of his forebears that Catholics were heretics and that only Moscow, the third Rome, had preserved the "pure religion" in its integrity.[6]

Sophia Wins

Feodor II (1676–1681) was well disposed toward Western ideas, because of his great admiration for his former tutor, Simeon of Polotsk. In 1680 Czar Feodor married a young lady of Polish origin, who was said to have Catholic leanings. With the encouragement of the Czar, Simeon of Polotsk founded in Moscow a rudimentary university. Immediately afterwards the sovereign's beloved friend died. Then Patriarch Joachim said that he wished no monks from Kiev to serve as teachers in the Muscovite Academy. Feodor II accordingly sent to Constantinople for professors, but the sickly young ruler did not live to witness the arrival of the Greek monks in Moscow.[7]

Patriarch Joachim and the principal boyars had decided

that the hardy Peter should be placed on the throne, because the deceased Czar's brother, the feeble-minded Ivan, was not fit to rule. Natalia Naryshkin would act as regent, for her son was not yet ten years of age. But the six daughters of Czar Alexis by his first wife were not prepared to accept the victory of the Naryshkins. Sophia, the most brilliant of the Miloslavsky princesses, had friends among the *streltsi,* or palace guard.

With their aid the ambitious princess inspired a riot. During the rising a number of Natalia's close relatives were murdered. These acts of violence took place before the eyes of the young Peter, who never forgot them. On May 23, 1682, a council of boyars, intimidated by the pikes of the palace guard, decided that both boys should reign as Czars. The precedence was accorded to Ivan, with the title of sovereign Czar. The regency passed to Sophia.

Sophia Miloslavsky had an abundance of learning, brains, and boldness. Her principal minister and favorite, the handsome and cultured Basil Galitzin, directed her foreign policy. Galitzin desired friendly relations with the West, advised the boyars to send their sons to study in European universities, and believed that ministers of foreign faiths should have permission to reside in Russia.

Austria Sponsors a Jesuit Mission

Leopold I of Austria was anxious to enlist Russia in the struggle against the Turks. In 1684 he sent an embassy to Moscow. A Jesuit, Father John Schmidt, served as chaplain of the Austrian embassy. The devout Emperor Leopold was prepared to do everything possible to promote the reunion of Russia and Rome and to safeguard the position of foreign Catholics in Moscow.

Just then a break had occurred in Russo-Polish relations, so Basil Galitzin told the Austrian envoys that the Emperor would have to negotiate peace between Russia and Poland, before

Moscow would consider war against Turkey. The Austrian ambassadors were not empowered to represent Poland in such negotiations, and a stalemate resulted.

At this point Leopold I sent an Italian Jesuit, disguised as a nobleman, to serve as chaplain to the principal imperial envoy in Moscow. This Father Carlo Vota had long talks with Basil Galitzin about the union of the Churches. Permission was at length accorded to Father Schmidt to remain in Moscow as imperial missioner and chaplain to the foreign Catholics, but Galitzin would not commit the agreement to writing. Emperor Leopold undertook to finance the mission in Moscow.

The next envoy sent northward by the persistent Emperor was Hans Kurtz, one of his most skilled diplomats. A Jesuit, Father Albert de Boye, went with Kurtz. The imperial ambassador did not succeed in persuading the Russians to make war on Turkey, but he did secure permission for Father de Boye to remain in Moscow. From then until 1689 there were always two Jesuit missioners in the Russian capital. The majority of the Russian clergy, and especially the Patriarch Joachim, were bitterly opposed to the presence of Jesuits in their midst.

The Jesuits ministered to about one hundred Catholic families in the foreign suburb of Moscow. The leader of the little Catholic community was Patrick Gordon, a Scottish General. Later, when Peter the Great assumed control, he admitted the Catholic Gordon into his intimate friendship. Besides ministering to the foreign Catholics in Moscow, the Jesuits opened a school. Some courageous boyars sent their children to the Catholic institution.

The Greek professors requested by Czar Feodor arrived in Moscow, and they soon stirred up a lively controversy as to the exact moment when the bread and wine are changed into the Body and Blood of Christ in the Sacrifice of the Mass. On one side were the Jesuits and a number of Russians who were attracted to Catholic ideas. The Patriarch and the Greek monks led the opposite party. The war of books and pamphlets continued as long as Sophia was regent.

Through their school the Jesuits established secret contacts with the relatives of their Muscovite pupils. A few boyars became Catholics, and a greater number were drawn to the Church without daring to take the final step. The propaganda of the Jesuits also reached a few members of the clergy. But the Catholic missioners, confined as they were to the foreign suburb and closely watched, were quite unable to reach the Russian masses.[8]

Sophia is Found Wanting

In 1686 Basil Galitzin concluded with Poland a treaty whereby the Poles ceded Kiev to Russia, in return for the Muscovite promise to join in the war against Turkey. The following year the infatuated Sophia urged Galitzin to march against the Tartars of the Crimea, allies of Turkey. But the Russian troops returned without glory in the autumn, and with thousands missing. In Moscow such anger rose against the unsuccessful Galitzin, that a man of the people tried to stab Sophia's minister.

Basil Galitzin undertook a second expedition against the Tartars in 1689. It turned out only a little better than the first. Sophia would not admit defeat; she insisted that her favorite head a victory parade in the Red Square. The parade, without Tartar prisoners and with decimated Russian ranks, angered the spectators. The Muscovites weighed Sophia in their minds and found wanting this princess who had so boldly emerged from the time-honored seclusion of highborn Russian women.

During the regency of Sophia, Peter and his mother had lived in isolation at Transfiguration Village, near Moscow. Peter, an exceptionally tall and strong boy, had received little formal education, but he read widely and was a born technician. At Transfiguration he learned some Latin, German, and Dutch. The boy Czar drilled his playmates into a little army and requisitioned military equipment from the palace arsenal. His "battalion of playmates" maneuvered after the European fashion and became the kernel of his future regular army.

Transfiguration Village was not far from Moscow's foreign suburb, and Peter soon became acquainted with some of the leading Westerners. A Dutchman, Christian Brandt, built a boat for the young Czar and showed him how to sail it. Peter navigated his craft on Pereiaslav Lake and dreamed of future naval victories. In 1689 Natalia arranged a marriage for her son with Eudokia Lapukhin, who had been reared according to the ancient Muscovite traditions. It was a union foredoomed to failure.

Sophia became alarmed by her half-brother's military and naval games. She instigated a plot to murder Natalia, but Peter was warned and he took sanctuary in the famous Monastery of the Trinity. There he was joined by the leading boyars, by many Russian regiments, and finally by the *streltsi* themselves. On September 12, 1689, Peter marched on Moscow and relegated Sophia to a convent. Peter was gentle with his feeble-minded half brother Ivan, who died in peaceful retirement in 1696.

Basil Galitzin received an order in writing, signed by Peter himself. It read: "You are commanded by the Czar to betake yourself far away, beneath the Arctic, and to stay there all your days." Thus the Jesuits in Moscow lost their protector, and Peter was deprived of the services of a truly superior Russian.[9]

Banishment of the Jesuits

Patriarch Joachim lost no time in attacking the Catholic missioners. Two prominent Russians, sympathetic to the Jesuits, were executed. On October 12, 1689, the Jesuits themselves were ordered to leave Moscow within forty-eight hours. But the triumph of the reactionaries among the Russian clergy was brief. Patriarch Joachim died in 1690. Four years later the Greek monks were dismissed from Russia, and in 1702 the Moscow Academy was entrusted to monks from Kiev.

Emperor Leopold I tried in vain to reinstall the Jesuits in Moscow. A Dominican missioner served for a short while as chaplain of the foreign Catholics in the Russian capital. Then two Austrian secular priests were sent northward. After six years they asked to return to their native land, and their desire was granted in 1698. Their successors would be Jesuits.

Meanwhile a French Jesuit had aroused the ire of Peter the Great. Father Philip Avril had tried unsuccessfully to obtain permission to cross Siberia on his way to China. In 1692 Father Avril published a book in which he said Czar Peter was subject to epilepsy, a disease hereditary among the Romanovs. The book reached Moscow and the young ruler was furious. "It is no longer possible to count on Peter's good will toward the Catholics," warned the alarmed General Patrick Gordon.[10]

Footnotes to Chapter Six

[1] Donald Attwater, *The Catholic Eastern Churches,* p. 78.
[2] Ivan Gagarin, *The Russian Clergy,* pp. 101 f.
[3] Gregor Alexinsky, *Russia and Europe,* pp. 27–29.
[4] Helen Iswolsky, *Soul of Russia,* pp. 45–55.
[5] G. P. Fedotov, editor, *A Treasury of Russian Spirituality,* pp. 134–81.
[6] Paul Pierling, *La Russie et le Saint-Siège.* Vol. IV, pp. 48–75.
[7] Ivan Gagarin, *op. cit.,* pp. 103 ff.
[8] Paul Pierling, *op. cit.* Vol. IV, pp. 77–106.
[9] K. Waliszewski, *Pierre Le Grand,* pp. 54 f.
[10] Paul Pierling, *op. cit.* Vol. IV, pp. 110–23.

CHAPTER SEVEN

Yury Krijanitch

IN THE time of Czar Alexis and of Czar Feodor II a remarkable Catholic missioner was in Russia, but he spent the greater part of his apostolate in Siberian exile. Yury Krijanitch was born near the town of Zagreb, Croatia, about the year 1618. The gifted boy was proud of his Slav origin and he suffered from the dependent condition of Croatia. In the lifetime of Krijanitch the Croats were oppressed by German military rule.

The Bishop of Agram sent the promising youth to study theology in Vienna and in Bologna. In the latter city the Croatian seminarian read Antonio Possevino's writings on Moscow, and any other available books about Russia. Thus Yury Krijanitch discovered his vocation and dedicated himself irrevocably to the work of uniting the principal people of the Slav race to Rome. Moscow and Rome became henceforth the two poles of his laborious life.

In order to prepare himself for his lifework Krijanitch went to Rome and was admitted to the Greek College of St. Athanasius in 1641. In this college, under the jurisdiction of the Sacred Congregation for the Propagation of the Faith, Jesuit professors trained Greek and Slav seminarians for missionary work among Eastern peoples. Before his ordination to the priesthood Krijanitch submitted a memoir to the Sacred Congregation of the Propagation of the Faith.

In this memoir the Croat revealed himself as one of the earliest exponents of Pan-Slavism. He desired that all the Slav peoples should unite under the hegemony of Russia, because he thought that only in this way would they be strong enough to assert their independence. Krijanitch maintained that, whereas pride had separated the Greeks from Rome, the Russians were victims of their own ignorance. Enlightenment would suffice to reunite them to the Holy See. He was opposed to all attempts to latinize the Russian Church. His point of view concerning the Eastern rite is now the official policy of the Vatican.

Krijanitch asked to be sent to Russia in the character of a man of letters and a scientist. He hoped thus to enter the Russian ruler's service. At the opportune time the missioner disguised as a savant would exhort the Czar to achieve glory by defending Christendom against the Turks, at the same time stressing the need of religious union with the West in order to cement military solidarity. "And when the stage of discussing religious union will have been reached, then may the merciful Lord deign to direct all things to His honor and glory," wrote the zealous lover of Rome and Russia.[1]

An Impatient Man

The Sacred Congregation for the Propagation of the Faith took note of the Croat's apostolic desires, and filed his memoir. Krijanitch was ordained to the priesthood in 1642; toward the close of the same year he returned to Croatia to serve in the diocese of Agram. But the young priest thought ceaselessly of Russia. Bishop Parczewski, of Smolensk, was asking for new helpers, so in 1646 Krijanitch was assigned to that diocese.

At that time Smolensk was still under Polish domination, but it would be retaken by the Russians eight years later.

The delighted Croat thought himself on the direct road to Moscow, but his joy was of short duration. Bishop Parczewski followed the Latin rite and paid little attention to the Uniates among his flock. The prelate thought his new assistant was an unbalanced visionary and he took an immediate dislike to the young priest. To rid himself of the troublesome missioner Bishop Parczewski allowed Krijanitch to become the chaplain of a Polish magnate.

Krijanitch had little patience. When an opportunity of accompanying a Polish embassy to Moscow presented itself, he left for the Russian capital without the permission of his religious superiors. He spent two months in the city of his desires toward the close of the year 1647. It is probable that the Croat had an interview with Patriarch Joseph and that he called on Feodor Rtistchev, the enlightened majordomo of Czar Alexis.

In Moscow, Krijanitch somehow obtained a copy of the *Book of Cyril,* which had been compiled at the request of Czar Michael in order to furnish the Orthodox with arguments against "heretics and dissidents." This extraordinary work was full of the most ridiculous errors, and Krijanitch felt that he was the man to refute them. The Croat wrote to the Congregation for the Propagation of the Faith, proposing himself for this task, but received as answer a request to send the *Book of Cyril* to Rome. It was too much to ask, and it is probable that Krijanitch did not part with his treasure.

Flight to Moscow

After having left Moscow with the Polish embassy, Krijanitch went to Vienna. In 1651 he served as chaplain of an Austrian embassy to Constantinople. The following year found the Croat once more in Rome, where he translated into Latin the writings of twelve schismatical authors quoted in the *Book of Cyril.* Rome valued the erudition of the Croatian priest, but found that his character lacked balance. He had "a confused and extravagant mind" and could not be counted upon, the authorities decided.[2]

In 1658 Pope Alexander VII granted Krijanitch a pension, in appreciation of the missioner's literary work. But just then the Croat heard that the Muscovites were about to establish courses in philosophy. Surely a signal opportunity was at hand for the enlightenment of the Russians! Krijanitch begged the Pope to dispatch a legate to Moscow and to send him along as interpreter. As the Vatican showed no hurry to follow the Croat's advice, apostolic impatience once again got the better of Krijanitch. He packed his papers and his books and stole off secretly in the direction of Moscow.

Krijanitch reached the Russian capital in September, 1659, and at first he was well received as a Western savant eager to serve Moscow. Czar Alexis granted him a pension and he was ordered to prepare a Slav grammar and dictionary. "They call me a wanderer, but this is not true. I have come to the Czar of my race, to my own people, to the only country where my works can be utilized and do some good," wrote the jubilant missioner.[3]

At this time the schism caused by Patriarch Nikon's reforms had already swept Muscovy. Krijanitch saw in the Patriarch the symbol of unity as opposed to the people's obscurantist and anarchical tendencies, so he wrote a treatise defending Nikon. This defense must have been pleasing to the highest Muscovite authorities, but there is no evidence that the Croat ever achieved the happiness of an audience with Czar Alexis.

Siberian Exile

Krijanitch had been only sixteen months in his dear Moscow, when an ukase of January 20, 1661 exiled him to Tobolsk in Siberia. Did the blow fall without warning? Only surmises are possible. In a memoir presented to the Congregation for the Propagation of the Faith toward the close of his life the Croat said that during his stay of 1659–1661 in Moscow he was in touch with crypto-Catholics. Perhaps an indiscretion of one of those secret Catholics had something to do with the Latin missioner's sudden disgrace.

In any case, Krijanitch was quickly hustled out of Moscow. He was to remain fifteen years among the Russians, Poles, Lithuanians, Swedes, Germans, and Old Believers who peopled Tobolsk, most of whom were exiles or prisoners of war. In Tobolsk the Catholic missioner asked the blessing of a fellow exile, the Archpriest Avvakum, but the rigid Old Believer would not grant it. Then Krijanitch said, "If you do not wish to bless me, God blesses me. May you, too, remain with God." [4]

The Croat continued to receive a pension, and he was allowed to pursue his literary labors. Krijanitch was the first to develop the idea that Russia is Eurasian, and that she should serve as a link between the civilizations of the West and of the East. He wrote a valuable book on Siberia, and a volume about Russian traffic with China.

The most important works written by Krijanitch in Siberia were his *Politica* and his *De Providentia Dei.* In these treatises the Catholic priest developed his fundamental idea: the reunion of Russia with Rome. These writings also afford a realistic picture of seventeenth-century Muscovy, and a glimpse into the glorious future foreseen by the Croat for Russia. Though Krijanitch desired that Russia should seek lessons from the West, he warned that she must not become denationalized. The missioner wrote of foreigners in Muscovy: "They fool us and lead us by the nose. They think they are like gods and we are like fools." [5]

Krijanitch was by no means blind to Russia's faults. He enumerated the political and economic reforms which he considered urgent. "Our great misfortune is our lack of moderation in the exercise of power," he said, identifying himself with the people of his predilection. "We have no sense of measure. We go to extremes and wander on the brink of precipices." [6]

It is known that Sophia's prinicpal minister, the able Basil Galitzin, owned copies of the works of Krijanitch. Russian historians tell us that young Czar Peter one day discovered the *Politica* and the *De Providentia Dei* "somewhere in the attic." Certain reforms of Peter the Great have a striking likeness to those suggested by the Catholic Croatian exile in Siberia.

With Vision Undimmed

After Krijanitch had suffered a serious illness in Siberia, he begged Czar Alexis to put an end to his exile. He was informed that he would be pardoned if he renounced Catholicism. Instead, the brave apostle wrote a book in which he openly urged the Czar to reunite the Russian Church with the Holy See. So, Krijanitch remained in Tobolsk until the accession to the throne of the young Czar Feodor II, who pardoned the Catholic missioner. Krijanitch left the place of his long exile in March, 1676.

The Russians urged the Western savant to remain in Moscow, but Krijanitch felt that his apostolate was compromised by the fact that everyone now knew he was a Catholic priest. The Croat obtained permission to leave Muscovy in October, 1677, and the following year he took an amazing step. Krijanitch entered the Dominican Order in Vilna. It was a mistake, because his temperament did not fit him for community life.

The new Dominican soon perceived his mistake, so he endeavored vainly to be released from his vows. He wished to acquaint Rome with the fruits of his painful years in the realm of Czar Alexis. In a touching letter to the Congregation for the Propagation of the Faith, written in 1682, the old missioner recognized that he had done wrong in setting forth for

Moscow without perimssion. He could only ask pardon, with "tears of blood." [7]

Rome ordered the Croat's superiors to send him to the Eternal City, and Krijanitch set out on foot on his last journey. He arrived in Vienna in September, 1683, when the Turks were besieging the city. The missioner who had suffered so many failures and disappointments, achieved grandeur in the manner of his death. He was slain in the ranks of the Polish army, while ministering to the wounded and the dying. In the lifetime of Yury Krijanitch, the fertility and truth of his ideas were not appreciated, but today he is universally recognized as a brave and gifted apostolic precursor.

Footnotes to Chapter Seven

[1] Paul Pierling, *La Russie et le Saint-Siège.* Vol. IV, p. 13.
[2] *Ibid.,* p. 22.
[3] Helen Iswolsky, *Soul of Russia,* pp. 61 f.
[4] Paulin-Gérard Scolardi, *Krijanich,* p. 128.
[5] Yury Krijanitch, *On Foreigners.* Leo Wiener's *Anthology of Russian Literature.* Vol. I, pp. 134–36.
[6] Helen Iswolsky, *op. cit.,* p. 63.
[7] Paulin-Gérard Scolardi, *op. cit.,* p. 149.

CHAPTER EIGHT

Peter and Religious Union

PETER FORESAW the usefulness of friendly relations with the Holy See. He was therefore pleased when one of his great boyars and devoted servitors, Boris Sheremetev, expressed a desire to visit Rome. The great boyar arrived in Rome in 1698, accompanied by his majordomo, Alexis Kurbatov, a leading Russian financier. Sheremetev was granted an audience by Pope Innocent XII. He seemed to be on the point of joining the Catholic Church, and Kurbatov actually did so. But on their return to Russia, both men were caught up in the whirlwind activity of Peter the Great, and their visit to Rome was without durable results.[1]

In 1695 the young Czar resumed Sophia's war with Turkey. The following year he took the Turkish fortress of Azov, on the sea of the same name. Peter at once began to construct harbors on the neighboring coast and launched a huge shipbuilding program.

On the advice of his clever Swiss friend, Franz Lefort, Peter set out on a journey of education to Europe in 1697. An embassy was formed, with Lefort as its nominal head. The purpose of the embassy was to persuade the Western nations to enlist in a crusade against Turkey. The Czar traveled with the embassy incognito, under the name of Peter Mikhailov. He intended to bring back to Russia a great number of foreign experts to instruct his backward people.

Peter Amazes Europe

The Russian ruler was six feet eight inches tall, and under his gusty good humor lurked savagery. His energy was almost intolerable. Like a thunderbolt he hurtled about, swinging his long arms as he moved. Anger sometimes flashed from his fine, intelligent eyes and then his handsome face twitched with a convulsive tic. Already the young autocrat was determined to make his country a European Power by "reforming" it on the model of the West. He was prepared to proceed by trial and error, not counting the cost in human life and suffering. "He is very bad and very good," wrote the astute Electress of Hanover.[2]

The young Czar worked as a common shipwright on the wharves of Holland, and he enlisted nearly a thousand experts of various kinds for the service of Russia. In England Peter watched a sham naval battle off Spithead, a spectacle he never forgot. At Vienna Leopold I, the protector of the Catholic mission in Moscow, was eager to win the Czar's friendship. Peter discussed religious union with the Jesuits, and assisted at Catholic services. The favorable reports from Vienna aroused enthusiastic hopes in Rome, but the Russian ruler was not to visit Italy.

In Vienna Peter received word that the palace guard, egged on by ex-Regent Sophia, had revolted in his absence. The Czar returned hurriedly to Russia by way of Poland. In the latter country Peter promised the Papal Nuncio that missioners to the Orient would be allowed to pass through Moscow, but the Czar would not put his promise in writing, saying that his word was worth more than a scrap of paper.

On his arrival in Moscow, Peter ordered his courtiers to wear European clothes and to shave off their cherished beards. He took a terrible vengeance on the palace guard, who had served as the tools of all the partisans of Old Russia. The Czar beheaded five of the *streltsi* with his own hand. The executions lasted seven days and a thousand victims were put to death. Sophia was moved to a narrow cell and shorn of her hair. She lived for four more years. Peter's wife, Eudokia Lapukhin, was found guilty of siding with the Czar's enemies. The unfortunate woman was forced to enter a convent, but the masses continued to consider her as the lawful Czarina.

Jesuits Again in Moscow

In 1698 Leopold I sent to Moscow an experienced career diplomat, Ignatius de Guarient. Guarient took with him two Jesuits, Father John Milan and Father John Berula, who passed as Austrian diocesan priests, and a Veronese missioner, Father Casagrande. When Guarient arrived in Moscow, Peter was still abroad. The temporary government allowed the two Jesuits to install themselves in the foreign suburb, while Father Casagrande was sent to minister to the Venetians working at the Voronezh wharves on the Don River.

On his return to Russia Peter refused to stabilize the position of the imperial missioners in Moscow. He was displeased with Leopold I, because Austria had concluded a truce with Turkey. When Catholic missioners asked to journey to China by way of Siberia, the Czar refused their request. He referred to his promise to the Papal Nuncio in Poland as mere "table talk."

The Jesuits reopened their school. They won a few converts among the boyars and the clergy, but for reasons of secrecy the names of these neophytes were not recorded. Patriarch Adrian died in 1700. The patriarchal duties, shorn of the title, fell to Stephen Yavorsky, who had studied with the

Uniates at Vilna. At first Yavorsky appeared friendly to the Jesuits, but he became jealous because the Jesuit school was superior to any of his.

A Russian deacon, Peter Artemiev, had been converted by a priest of the first Jesuit mission in Moscow. Now he began openly to preach Catholic doctrine. The intrepid young confessor of the Faith was imprisoned for life in Solovetsky Monastery, on the White Sea. On the other hand, Orthodox boyars and clergy were permitted to engage freely in religious discussions with the Jesuits. But the friendship of Peter was absolutely necessary for the attainment of any security.

In 1699 Peter was much affected by the death of General Patrick Gordon. When Gordon for the last time recommended to Peter the Catholic community in Moscow, the Czar told him, "Have no anxiety, little father." Peter gave his friend a magnificent funeral, and the elite of the Russian nation assisted at the Catholic ceremonies. The Jesuits' teaching activities corresponded perfectly with Peter's desires for the education of Russia, so the Czar turned a deaf ear to those who attacked the Catholic school.[3]

Wanton Murder

Peter desired to open a "window into Europe" for Russia on the Baltic coast, almost all of which was then in the possession of Sweden. In 1700 the Czar accordingly joined a coalition of Poland and Denmark against the young Charles XII of Sweden, a soldier of genius. During the struggle with Charles, which lasted nine years, Peter had urgent need of the Pope's intervention in Poland, so he spoke openly of the union of the Churches.

Charles XII forced Denmark to retire from the coalition. Then he marched against Peter and defeated the Czar's ill-trained and ill-supplied troops at Narva. Next, the Swedish ruler turned aside to bring Poland to her knees. With indomitable courage Peter made use of this respite for the work of military organization. He sailed down the clear, blue Neva River to its mouth, captured a small fort, and renamed it St. Petersburg. In a flash of genius the young Czar determined that this fortress on a Finnish marsh should one day be transformed into the new capital of Russia.

It was during this period that Peter took as his second wife a young servant girl made prisoner by the Russian troops in Livonia. Renamed Catherine, the former servant girl thereafter shared all Peter's interests. When the Czar fell victim to one of his terrible rages, Catherine was the only person who could soothe his black fury, by patiently stroking his shaking head.

At this time Peter also ordered his representative in Austria, Prince Galitzin, to issue an ultimatum to the Vatican. Rome must give an answer within a month's time concerning the matter of the reunion of the Churches, otherwise the Czar intended to come to an understanding with the Lutherans! Since Peter had never made any definite proposition concerning the union, this ultimatum was, to say the least, stupefying. Prince Galitzin had the good sense to let the matter drop, but the affair was not reassuring as to the Czar's stability.

Meanwhile Charles XII had been winning victories in Poland, and Peter went to the aid of his ally. As the Czar's troops advanced into Polish territory, they persecuted the Uniate clergy; it was even rumored that Peter himself was destroying statues of Saint Josaphat Kuncevich. On the morning of July 11, 1705, Peter appeared at the Basilian monastery in Polotsk. He had been drinking all night at an official banquet. As soon as the Czar entered the monastery he saw a statue of the Uniate saint. A Basilian monk had come to greet the dread visitor, and Peter asked him who had killed Archbishop Kuncevich.

The Basilian replied that "schismatics" had slain the martyr. Infuriated by the fatal word, the impulsive Peter drew his sword and slaughtered the Catholic priest. Four other Basilians who hastened to the aid of their confrere were likewise slain, either by the Czar himself or by his officers. After that the monastery was given over to pillage, the surviving Basilians were thrown into prison, and military supplies were stored in the Uniate cathedral. Some months later, Peter said that he regretted his action and he promised to protect the Uniates.[4]

Peter Has Recourse to Rome

Charles XII again defeated Peter at Grodno in the spring of 1706. Then the young Swedish conqueror forced Augustus II of Poland to renounce his crown, but Peter hoped to reinstall his ally on the Polish throne. The intervention of the Pope in Poland could prove decisive, so the Czar did not hesitate to have recourse to it.

Peter sent as his ambassador to the Vatican his brother-in-law, the handsome and well-educated Boris Kuragin. Prince Kuragin was definitely hostile to Catholicism, but he was most courteous in all his dealings with the Vatican. The keen Pope Clement XI perceived plainly that the Czar's aim was political rather than religious. The negotiations had no definite result, because in his brief the Pope did not accord Peter the title of "Majesty." The Czar, therefore, refused to accept the papal document, and Prince Kuragin later said that never afterwards did Peter think of becoming a Catholic.

Glorious Poltava

After Charles XII had driven King Augustus II to the wall, he was free to turn against Peter. The Swedish conqueror plunged into Russia and made the mistake of descending southward to winter among the Dnieper Cossacks, because their leader had offered his traitorous allegiance to Charles. The winter of 1708–1709 was a terrible one in Russia. It wrought havoc with the Swedish ruler's troops and supplies. On June 27, 1709, Peter advanced to join battle with Charles XII at Poltava. The Czar's famous order before the encounter read: "Do not think of Peter, the only thing that matters is that Russia remain alive!" At Poltava the brave Swedes were defeated.[5]

Now that Peter had won his great victory at Poltava, he had no further urgent need of friendly relations with the Vatican. In 1714 Father Milan wrote from the Jesuit mission in Moscow: "Unless a first class miracle occurs, there is no hope that Czar Peter will come to an understanding with the Vatican. Peter would have to submit to the authority of the Pope, and to moral laws. He would have to renounce his whims and his abuses of power." [6]

The foreign Catholics in Russia continued to enjoy religious liberty, but the Uniates in Lithuania suffered endless vexations from the Russian troops. Rome suffered agony because of the persecuted Uniates, but could find no means of establishing relations with St. Petersburg.

Racing Against the Wind

After Poltava, Peter turned his attention with more concentrated energy to reforms at home. He transformed a disorderly medieval levy into a conquering modern army. He established schools for the education of his gentry. Peter's Russia was a preview of the modern totalitarian State, in which every part must be sacrificed to the greatness of the whole. His helpers were the men who could most effectively carry out his orders, and they obeyed him without question. Rank and nobility were made to depend on service to the State, not on birth.

The Czar introduced a new Russian alphabet, corrected and simplified. He issued ukases to correct the social behavior of his subjects. These orders make enjoyable reading, because

Peter had a genius for pithy statement. Peter I was the founder of Russian industry, and he promoted it with all the authority of the State. The Czar appointed government agents to detect any financial corruption, but the resulting spying and informing did not improve the honesty of Russian officials.

Peter's reforms meant added financial burdens for the masses. The new poll tax was a sore vexation to the peasants. In order to found his new Empire, the Czar had to leave conservative Moscow. Forty thousand peasants labored, suffered, and often died in the noxious marshes to construct the buildings and the canals of St. Petersburg. Peter liked the peasants and enjoyed stopping in their cottages, but he recognized serfdom as something which he could not replace within the span of his lifetime. Fugitive serfs were treated as criminals, and annual man-hunts to recover the runaways were organized with full government authority.

In his haste to abolish the traditional seclusion of highborn Russian women the Czar manifested the impatience that characterized all his reforms. As Klyuchevsky wrote, "By racing against the wind, Peter increased its velocity against him." The quiet man was everywhere resentful and disturbed.

Peter at the Sorbonne

Peter had not visited France during his early travels in Europe, so in 1717 he satisfied his curiosity about Paris. While examining the mechanism of the fountains in the Trianon gardens, the Czar sprayed water over the elegantly garbed assemblage of guests. In those years the Sorbonne was infested with Jansenism. Peter visited the venerable university, and the professors who welcomed him were Jansenists. They seized the opportunity of discussing religious union with the Czar.

Peter proposed that the doctors prepare a memoir for the Russian bishops. The heretics accordingly compiled a memoir which was an extraordinary mixture of truth and error. On his return to Russia the Czar gave the memoir to the Orthodox bishops and ordered them to answer it. The Russian prelates obeyed Peter, but in their answer they evaded the issue by saying that they could not engage in a controversy of such importance without the knowledge and consent of all the Oriental Patriarchs.[7]

In 1718 all Peter's enemies rallied around the Czarevitch Alexis, the son of the unhappy Eudokia Lapukhin. The religious and peace-loving nature of Alexis was completely out of sympathy with his father's radical changes. Pursued through the years by Peter's reproaches and anger, Alexis finally fled to Austria. But Peter's agents found the fugitive, and by false promises persuaded him to return to Russia.

The accomplices of the Czarevitch's flight were examined under torture, and their confessions made it evident that Alexis had become the center of hope for all the disaffected. The terrified young man himself admitted that he had conspired against his father. The Czar submitted the fate of his son to the decision of the highest ecclesiastics and civil administrators in the land. On June 26, 1718 it was announced that the Czarevitch was no more.[8]

End of the Jesuit Mission

By 1719 the friendship between Austria and Russia had cooled to the point where connection with Austria proved the undoing of the Jesuits in Russia. By then St. Petersburg, as well as Moscow, had two resident Jesuit missioners. The Jesuits took long journeys to minister to foreign Catholics in Narva, Abo, Archangel, Voronezh, Kazan, Astrakhan, and Azov. In April, 1719 Peter abruptly terminated all this apostolic activity by an edict of expulsion. He said that he had permitted the Jesuits to remain in Russia only in order to please the Emperor, and now this consideration no longer existed.

The Jesuits left in Russia some two thousand Catholics.

Among those Catholics were a few Russian converts whose names are unknown: a bishop, three priests, and twenty-five boyars. The Jesuits never again came as a community to Moscow, though they did at times return there individually.[9]

In 1721, after Peter had concluded a highly advantageous peace with Sweden, the senate hailed him by the name of Peter the Great, and the title of Emperor was conferred on him and his successors. During that same year Peter abolished the Russian Patriarchate, reducing the national Church to a mere cog in the governmental machine. The Patriarch was replaced by the Holy Synod, a gathering of clergy selected by the autocrat. The latter ruled the Synod by means of its Procurator General, a layman who served as the "Czar's eyes and ears." Peter passed severe laws against the monasteries, which had stanchly opposed his reforms.

After the expulsion of the Jesuits from Russia, the Congregation for the Propagation of the Faith replaced them by Conventuals and Capuchins. The impulsive Peter soon wearied of these new Catholic missioners. Toward the close of the year 1724 he urged both groups to leave Russia. He was planning to replace them by Dominican missioners, but death did not permit the autocrat to take decisive steps.[10]

The Mighty Struggle Ends

Peter had not ceased to worry about the permanence of his beloved reforms. He decreed that the Russian sovereign should henceforth have the right to name his successor; but this ruling availed Peter nothing, because he died suddenly during the night of January 27–28, 1725. He had ordered the construction of a movable chapel beside his sickbed, and in it was placed the icon with which he had always traveled.

Klyuchevsky wrote of Peter's feverish endeavor to Europeanize Russia by the knout: "He hoped through the threat of his authority to evoke initiative in an enslaved society, and through slave-owning nobility to introduce into Russia European science and popular education as the necessary condition of social initiative. He desired that the slave, remaining a slave, should act consciously and freely. The inter-action of despotism and freedom, of education and slavery, this is the political squaring of the circle."[11]

If Peter the Great had tried to force the union of the Churches upon the Russian people, in addition to his other bitterly resented reforms, it is a question if even his adamantine will could have prevailed. But Peter was not in earnest, because he had no real understanding of religion. As far as he was concerned, the union of the Churches was merely a convenient political bait to dangle before Rome. All his life, Peter's god was the Fatherland. Only at the end, as he gazed dumbly at the flickering of candlelight on his icon, did the mighty Czar sense dimly the Power of God.

Footnotes to Chapter Eight

[1] Paul Pierling, *La Russie et le Saint-Siège.* Vol. IV, pp. 129–37.
[2] Bernard Pares, *A History of Russia,* p. 188.
[3] Paul Pierling, *op. cit.* Vol. IV, pp. 144–64.
[4] *Ibid.* pp. 174–94.
[5] George Vernadsky, *A History of Russia,* p. 93.
[6] Paul Pierling, *op. cit.* Vol. IV, pp. 222–28.
[7] *Ibid.,* pp. 237–66.
[8] D. S. Merezhkovski, *Peter and Alexis,* in *A Treasury of Russian Literature,* edited by Bernard Guilbert Guerney, pp. 863–75.
[9] Paul Pierling, *op. cit.* Vol. IV, pp. 281–97.
[10] *Ibid.,* pp. 298–305.
[11] V. O. Klyuchevsky, *Course of Russian History,* Vol. IV, p. 282.

CHAPTER NINE

Jansenist Interlude

PETER THE GREAT left behind him a group of very able men who had been his co-workers. The devotion of some of these disciples to the memory of their former master's greatness was such as to insure the survival of Peter's reforms. This would be so in spite of the military and financial burdens under which the nation was then groaning.

Peter was succeeded by his widow, Empress Catherine I. During the seventeen months of her reign, the former servant girl wasted huge sums on her personal expenses. The Russian Academy of Sciences, projected by Peter the Great, was opened in these months. As Catherine's rule was drawing to a close, a converted princess of the Dolgoruky family afforded the Sorbonne an opportunity of sending a Jansenist apostle to Russia.

How a Jansenist Reached Moscow

While Prince Sergius Dolgoruky, the husband of Princess Irina, was serving as ambassador at The Hague, the Russian princess came under Jansenist influence. She never realized that her new spiritual guides were in disobedience to the Holy See. Princess Irina and her children became Catholics at Leiden in 1727. On her return to Russia the princess desired a Catholic chaplain, whom she planned to introduce into her native land as the tutor of her children. The Jansenists in Holland asked the advice of the doctors of the Sorbonne.

The doctors assigned to this important post a certain Abbé Jubé, fanatically attached to Jansenist beliefs. When the Dolgoruky princess and her Jansenist chaplain arrived in Russia in 1728, Catherine I had died. Peter II, a boy barely twelve years of age and the son of the unfortunate Czarevitch Alexis, was on the throne. Peter II moved the imperial court back to Moscow, and he brought to his palace his grandmother, Eudokia Lapukhin, released at last from her thirty years' imprisonment.

Foreign Catholics continued to enjoy religious liberty, but the government was by no means so tolerant toward Russians who sought to become Catholics, or toward Catholic priests who tried to convert members of the Orthodox Church. Indeed, the tendency was to treat Russian converts to Catholicism as state criminals.

In order to render his position more safe, Abbé Jubé secured the protection of the Duke of Liria, Spanish ambassador in Russia. The Duke already had a chaplain for his embassy, a Dominican by the name of Bernard Ribera. Father Ribera engaged in written and spoken controversy with the Orthodox clergy. The Dominican's activities facilitated Jubé's access to ecclesiastical circles in Moscow. It would seem that several prominent members of the Russian clergy were attracted to the Jansenist apostle's ideas.[1]

The Masterful Anna Ivanovna

Peter II died of smallpox in January, 1730. The Russian

aristocracy summoned to the throne the niece of Peter the Great, Anna Ivanovna, the widowed and childless Duchess of Kurland. The boyars made an attempt to limit the power of the sovereign, but as soon as the masterful Anna was installed in the Kremlin, she secured the support of the Guard and with their aid was enthroned as an autocratic monarch. Empress Anna transferred the court again to St. Petersburg. During her reign (1730–1740) supreme power was given to her favorite, Ernest Biren, a German Calvinist.

Empress Anna made a display of her Orthodoxy, and Abbé Jubé understood that he was henceforth in danger. He no longer had the aid of Father Ribera, who had returned to Spain. Empress Anna found out about the conversion and the Catholic chaplain of Princess Irina Dolgoruky. Abbé Jubé was expelled from Russia in 1732. After the Jansenist priest had gone, the Empress banished from Moscow the whole family of Prince Sergius Dolgoruky. Before Princess Irina left for her country estate, Empress Anna sent for the convert, insulted her violently in public and slapped her in the face.

Empress Anna Ivanovna arranged with the Congregation for the Propagation of the Faith that there should be in Russia two prefectures apostolic for foreign Catholics, that of Moscow and that of St. Petersburg. This administrative measure prepared the way for the Catholic hierarchy which would be formed in the Empire under Catherine II.[2]

Anna continued Peter's educational reforms. During her rule Russia was victorious over Turkey. All Europe was impressed by the superb fighting qualities of Russia's troops. Empress Anna named as her successor Ivan, the infant son of her niece, who was princess of Brunswick-Lüneburg. Biren served as regent. But the Russian gentry were sick of German rule. By means of a military conspiracy, the infant Ivan VI was imprisoned and Elizabeth, the favorite daughter of Peter the Great, was set on the throne.

Empress Elizabeth and Catholicism

The tall, handsome Elizabeth reigned from 1741 to 1762. She did her best to carry on her father's program, and she had the sovereign gift of choosing and using able advisers. Already in Elizabeth's time the Russian gentry turned away from the culture of the petty German courts and began to look to France as the school of worldly elegance. At this time a remarkable linguist, man of letters, and scientist, Mikhail Lomonosov, rendered incalculable services to Russian scholarship. Lomonosov had studied abroad, but he was the son of a deep-sea fisherman of Archangel.[3]

Soon after her accession, Empress Elizabeth brought to Russia her nephew Peter from the duchy of Holstein. The unfortunate Peter, who was of infirm mind, had adopted the ideas of the new Prussian militarism and Frederick the Great was his idol. In 1744 Elizabeth married her nephew to Princess Sophia Augusta of Anhalt-Zerbst. This intelligent German princess came to Russia at the age of fourteen, and she was rechristened Catherine in the Orthodox Church. Catherine was soon aware that her husband was an idiot. The ambitious girl would have been glad to part with Peter, but not with the Russian crown.

Empress Elizabeth was deeply devoted to the Orthodox Church. In 1745 Princess Irina Dolgoruky, who had so courageously resisted the persecutions of Empress Anna, yielded to the pressure exercised on her family by Elizabeth. Together with her son and daughter, Princess Irina publicly abjured Catholicism. Afterwards the unfortunate princess was most unhappy. She asked permission to live abroad, but she was refused a passport. Prominent members of the Russian clergy who had been friendly with Abbé Jubé and Father Ribera were imprisoned or executed.[4]

Elizabeth disliked Frederick the Great of Prussia, so she formed an alliance with France and Austria against him. The stubborn bravery of the Russian infantry won resounding victories over Frederick. In 1760 a Russian force of Cossacks and Tartars actually raided Berlin. Only the death of Empress Elizabeth saved Frederick the Great from ruin.

Catherine II "Accepts" the Throne

When Peter III succeeded his aunt in 1762, he proclaimed some welcome changes, but his personal conduct offended every Russian instinct. He concluded an alliance with Frederick the Great, and introduced the tedious Prussian drill into the Russian army. During Orthodox services he behaved disrespectfully; moreover, he threatened to divorce Catherine.

Catherine bided her time. At the opportune moment, a conspiracy in her behalf was set in motion by her numerous and able friends. Peter made an abject abdication. He was taken to the village of Ropsha by Catherine's troops. There he died on July 17, 1762, in the course of a scuffle with his custodians. Catherine declared in a manifesto that she accepted the throne to save the country, and she added that autocracy without the necessary qualities in the ruler is very dangerous. Two years after the murder of Peter III an attempt was made to free the deposed Ivan VI, imprisoned since 1741. The prison wardens put Ivan to death in order to prevent his liberation. Catherine then had no rival for the throne, except her own son, Paul Petrovitch.

Optimistic Worldliness

The chief characteristic of Catherine II was a certain optimistic worldliness. She did not like deep religious and philosophical questions. Though Catherine did her best to become Russian in her religion, as in all else, this did not prevent her from placing the domains of the national Church under the administration of the State.

The boundless ambition of the new Empress was not of the coldly calculating type. She was on the contrary sanguine, impetuous, fearless, and instinctively generous. She loved sudden changes and new beginnings. Catherine II was a woman of gracious majesty, with an agreeable voice and a gay laugh. She wrote of herself: "To tell the truth, I have never fancied myself extremely beautiful, but I had the gift of pleasing, and that, I think, was my greatest gift." [5]

In her private life the Empress had simple tastes. She worked in great bouts, like a Russian, full of enthusiasm for a project, until her interest in it waned. At different times the sovereign traveled widely in her vast domains, and each journey served as a course of self-education.

Catherine's letters to Frederick the Great, Emperor Joseph II, and the French Encyclopedists prove that she was a political genius. With consummate skill she kept herself and Russia in the world's news. She knew how to stimulate her helpers to action, and she did not listen to calumniators and detractors. Many of Catherine's ablest helpers were also her official favorites.

Catherine was a pupil of the French humanitarians. She became one of the "benevolent despots" of the period, blissfully unaware of the approaching storm of the French Revolution. She loved to write and her numerous letters are full of verve and intellect. In the reign of Catherine II an immense number of French books were translated into Russian. Her gentry began to swallow wholesale the political and social ideas which were then in vogue in Western Europe. At that time Freemasonry gained a strong hold in the Empire.

Wellsprings of Faith

The real Russia—made up of the stolid merchants, the country squires, and the peasant masses—was unaffected by the atheism of some of Catherine's courtiers. It might have been expected that the Orthodox Church would wilt away under the intensive secularization imposed on it by the government of Catherine II, but such was not the case. This secularization was aimed at reducing the monks to the status of mere government employees. But the monasteries, by returning to the mystical literature of the Eastern Fathers, were the first to inaugurate a powerful religious reaction in the Russian Church. Because the bishops were recruited from the monks, the whole Church was thus inevitably quickened by new spiritual life.

At this time lived Saint Tychon, who renounced the bishopric of Voronezh and retired into the solitude of a provincial monastery. Saint Tychon reflected in his rather complex spiritual life the Western Christian influences of the period, but in his voluntary poverty and his preference for the oppressed, he followed directly in the Russian traditions of Saint Theodosius and Saint Sergius.[6]

The Great Commission

When Catherine ascended the throne, Russia had long needed a new law code. For a year and a half the Empress labored at an *Instruction,* in which she said that serfdom ought to be rare and could be excused only by interests of the State. The *Instruction* completed, Catherine summoned to Moscow in 1766 a Great Commission of five hundred and sixty-four members from the whole Empire. The Empress followed the debates closely, and she herself was responsible for the thorough discussion of the question of serfdom.

But the debate on serfdom had no effective sequel. The gentry class had carried Catherine to power, and this Empress with no legitimate title to the throne could not afford to alienate her supporters. Consequently, in Catherine's time, the authority of the gentry over the peasants became more absolute than ever before. Millions of Russian serfs toiled painfully to wrest from nature the wherewithal to pay for Catherine's brilliant court.[7]

Catherine II endeavored to develop agriculture, roads, and canals. She invited German colonists to uninhabited lands along the Volga and in the Ukraine. In the reign of Catherine the Great, the daring Gregory Shelekhov was called "the Russian Columbus." He formed a trading company and occupied Kodiak Island near Alaska. From that base his company rapidly increased its holdings on the American continent itself.

In 1764 Catherine founded the celebrated Smolny Educational Institute for girls of good family. She opened the Public Library and a College of Medicine in St. Petersburg. The Empress herself set the example of inoculation against smallpox. While this German princess on the throne of Russia was thus carrying on the gigantic labors of Peter the Great, Providence had reserved for her a still more astounding role. By an imperial whim Catherine II was about to render an immense service to the Catholic Church.

Footnotes to Chapter Nine

[1] Paul Pierling, *La Russie et le Saint-Siège.* Vol. IV, pp. 308–53.
[2] *Ibid.*, pp. 358–406.
[3] Mikhail Vasilevich Lomonosov, *Letters to I. I. Shuvalov on Devotion to Science.* Leo Wiener's *Anthology of Russian Literature.* Vol. I, pp. 241–46.
[4] Paul Pierling, *op. cit.*, Vol. IV, pp. 377–405.
[5] K. Waliszewski, *The Romance of an Empress,* p. 310.
[6] St. Tychon of Zadonsk, *Letters,* in *A Treasury of Russian Spirituality,* edited by G. P. Fedotov, pp. 225–39.
[7] John Maynard, *Russia in Flux,* pp. 8 f.

CHAPTER TEN

Catherine and Paul Protect the Jesuits

CATHERINE II was in reality her own foreign minister. By means of personal correspondence with contemporary European sovereigns she carried on her brilliant and unscrupulous diplomacy. Catherine desired to take the Crimea from Turkey. She even dreamed of wresting Constantinople from the grip of the infidel. At this time the Russian alliance with Poland, begun in the reign of Czar Alexis, had become practically a protectorate. In 1763 Catherine and Frederick the Great placed on the Polish throne a puppet ruler, Stanislaus Poniatowski; in the following year Russia and Prussia concluded a treaty for common policy in the affairs of Poland.

The Poles rose in defense of their liberties, but they were defeated by the greatest of Russian generals, Alexander Suvorov. In the course of the fighting there was trouble along the Turkish frontier, so in 1768 Tartars of the Crimea invaded Russia. The Russians won repeated victories over the Tartars and the Turks, and Shagin Girei, a Russian protégé, was installed as khan in the Crimea. In his anxiety to curb Russian ambition, Frederick the Great made the unscrupulous suggestion that

Catherine should in the main take her compensation for her victories over the Turks not from Turkey, but from Poland.

Austria had to be brought into the deal to prevent her from assisting Turkey. On August 5, 1772, the three robber nations concluded a treaty of partition. By this first dismemberment five million of Poland's twelve million inhabitants passed under foreign domination. Russia seized territory around Polotsk, Vitebsk, and Minsk, the region known as White Russia.

Catherine II had decided to establish an archbishopric for the Latin Catholics in her domain. She spoke to the puppet ruler in Poland about the matter, and he ordered Massalski, Bishop of Vilna, to discover a suitable candidate for the office. As for the Uniate Catholics, Catherine regarded them as traitors to their ancestral faith. She established in the annexed territories a body of missionaries, accompanied by soldiers, whose duty it was to restore the Uniates to Orthodoxy.

Jesuits Under Russian Rule

As a consequence of the first dismemberment of Poland, four Jesuit colleges and two of the Fathers' residences passed under Russian rule. There were 201 Jesuits in those houses, 97 of whom were priests. The Empress revoked the ukase of 1719, by which Peter the Great had banished the Jesuits from Russia for all time. The Latin Catholics of Polotsk sent two Jesuits as their representatives to St. Petersburg to swear fidelity to the Empress. Catherine assured the Jesuits of her favor and protection.

On August 16, 1773, Pope Clement XIV signed the brief which suppressed the Society of Jesus. Catherine stated that she would not permit the promulgation of this brief in her Empire. She saw no one better equipped to teach youth than the Jesuits, she said. The Empress persisted in this attitude until her death. Consequently, the Society of Jesus was never suppressed in Russia.

Meanwhile the Polish ruler had presented a singular candidate for Catherine's approval as her new Latin archbishop. This Stanislaus Siestrzencewicz, originally a Lithuanian Calvinist, had become a Catholic in order to make a rich marriage, but the lady would still have none of him. The worldly Bishop Massalski took a fancy to the rejected suitor, and ordained him to the priesthood after only two months of theological studies.

Now Siestrzencewicz accepted the nomination of the Empress without waiting for the indispensable consent of the Vatican. In order to prevent a schism Clement XIV granted to Catherine's prelate the necessary jurisdiction. A man of the type of Siestrzencewicz could not be a sincere friend of the Jesuits, and he schemed again and again to promulgate the brief of suppression. But in this, the ambitious prelate had counted without his imperial mistress.[1]

In this same eventful year of 1773 Emelian Pugachev, a Cossack of the Don River, led a great rebellion which at one time spread to all eastern and southeastern Russia. Later the rising turned into a savage peasant war. Catherine's best generals at length put down the rebels, and Pugachev was executed at Moscow in January, 1775. No sooner had the gentry recovered from their terror of the recent tremendous explosion of popular anger, than they began to revert to their previous treatment of the serfs.

The Lightning Strikes

Pope Clement XIV died in 1774, and his successor, Pius VI, had always been a friend of the Jesuits. The new Pope granted the Jesuits in White Russia permission to receive into the Society former confreres living in other countries. In 1777 Catherine ordered Bishop Siestrzencewicz to ordain to the priesthood twenty Jesuit scholastics; two years later she commanded her prelate to authorize the opening of a Jesuit novitiate at Polotsk. In 1780 the Empress visited White Russia and showed marked favor to the Jesuits.

But though gracious to the Jesuits, Catherine exiled from Polotsk the Uniate archbishop, who had incurred her displeasure. Then the Empress wrote to the Pope, saying that she would present a worthy candidate for the vacant Uniate archbishopric if Pius VI, on his part, would authorize the erection of a Latin archbishopric in White Russia. The Russian sovereign desired that the Pope should appoint her prelate first archbishop of the new see of Mogilev, and that Siestrzencewicz should have as coadjutor Father Benislawski, a former Jesuit.

As time passed, Catherine tired of waiting for the outcome of Rome's slow diplomacy. The Papal Nuncio in Poland had acted as intermediary in the correspondence between Pope and Empress. Toward the close of 1782 he received a threatening ultimatum from Catherine II which caused him to write in his diary, "The lightning has struck!" Pius VI yielded for the good of the Church in Russia, and he wrote that he would send an envoy to St. Petersburg to carry out Catherine's wishes.

The imperious Russian ruler had already decided to forestall the Pope in the sending of an envoy. She chose Father Benislawski as her ambassador. He was to include in his requests the papal approval of the Society of Jesus in White Russia. Pius VI granted Catherine's requests concerning Archbishop Siestrzencewicz and Father Benislawski himself. Then, in the presence of several cardinals, the Pope raised his voice, saying, "I approve the Society of Jesus existing in White Russia. I approve it, I approve it." Catherine was pleased, and she acceded to the wishes of the Pope by nominating a candidate for the Uniate archbishopric of Polotsk.[2]

The year 1783 saw the fulfillment of another of Catherine's desires. Shagin, the puppet khan of Crimea, made over his dominion to the Empress, who did not hesitate to annex it. Catherine made a triumphant visit to the Crimea, taking with her all the foreign ambassadors. She had Suvorov and his soldiers gallop past her guests at the charge, exactly as in battle.

Progress of the Jesuits in Russia

Many former Jesuits from all over the world were readmitted to the Society in White Russia. Among them was Father Gruber, a distinguished scientist. At this time the Empress requested the Jesuits to introduce additional courses in science into their curriculum, so Father Gruber began immediately to train young Jesuits as professors for the new science courses. He also established courses in architecture and art for Jesuit lay brothers, and inaugurated textile and brewing industries on the Jesuit property at Polotsk. In 1785 Father Gruber was called to St. Peterburg, where he made the acquaintance not only of the foreign Catholics but also of prominent Russian gentry. At that period there were some ten thousand Catholics in Catherine's capital.

The Jesuits spread devotion to the Sacred Heart, preached retreats to the laity, visited the hospitals and the prisons, and accompanied the condemned to the scaffold. From each college the Fathers went out into the neighboring villages and towns to teach catechism. The Jesuits of White Russia also carried on mission work among the Letts in the region of Dagda.[3]

When the French Revolution broke out in 1789, Catherine's "liberalism" underwent a violent transformation. French books were excluded from Russia, and the Empress proclaimed that Europe was lost if it copied godless France. At the news that Louis XVI had been guillotined, Catherine fell seriously ill.

A Nation Without a Country

The unhappy Poles could not agree among themselves; in 1791 some of them appealed to Catherine II against their compatriots. The Russian troops entered Warsaw without difficulty. Then a Polish Diet was summoned to Grodno, surrounded by Russian soldiers, and forced to sanction a second partition in 1793. Prussia had made a deal with Russia, and secured territory in the heart of Poland. The victim of this second iniquity was left with a population of only four million.

At this time Catherine assumed for herself and her successors the obligation of "maintaining in perpetuity Catholics of both rites in the undisturbed possession of their prerogatives, property and churches, and in the free exercise of their cult and discipline." This solemn obligation was immediately disregarded. Between 1794 and 1796 more than a million and a half Uniates were forcibly incorporated into the Orthodox Church. The Empress suppressed all the Uniate dioceses, except that of Polotsk. She annihilated the order of Basilians, which had been the mainstay of Uniate Catholicism.[4]

In 1794 Poland made a last desperate bid for freedom, under the leadership of Thaddeus Kosciuszko, who had previously fought in the cause of American Independence. Three Russian armies thereupon entered Poland. The brave Kosciuszko was wounded and taken prisoner. After Suvorov had led an attack on Warsaw, Polish resistance collapsed. A terrible massacre reddened with blood the captured city. In October, 1795, Russia, Prussia, and Austria effected a third partition, by which Poland vanished from the map of Europe. Russia's share of the booty was Kurland and the rest of Lithuania.

Catherine's Greatest Service

The Empress had become certain that the rule of her son Paul could only prove disastrous for Russia, and she thought of replacing him in the succession by her favorite grandson, Alexander. She had personally supervised the beloved Alexander's education from his infancy. But Catherine died suddenly in November, 1796, without being able to name her successor. No sovereign since Ivan the Terrible had extended the frontiers of the Empire by such vast conquests as had Catherine II. She gave Russia for boundaries the Niemen, the Dniester, and the Black Sea.

Catherine the Great did not merely serve Russia. All Christendom is indebted to her for having protected and preserved the Society of Jesus. The Empress herself was not wholly unconscious of what she had done for the cause of Christianity. She wrote to the Encyclopedist Grimm, saying that she wondered if many of the evils of the French Revolution were not the result of the closing of the Jesuit schools. "The Jesuits cared well for the morals and the tastes of the young people, and whatever is best in France came out of their schools," said the stanch champion of the Society of Jesus in Russia.[5]

Evolution of a Tyrant

In his boyhood Paul knew that his mother did not love him, and he was afraid of her. A first marriage arranged by Catherine for her son with a German princess ended with the death of the young wife in 1776. A few months later the Empress brought to Russia as her new daughter-in-law another German princes, who was rechristened in the Orthodox Church as Maria Feodorovna. Paul's second wife was to bear him ten children.

In 1781 Paul made a journey to Western Europe in the company of his beloved Maria Feodorovna. He visited the Jesuits in White Russia, and he was received in Rome by Pope Pius VI. Paul spent hours in conversation with the Pope, and he conceived a warm affection for the head of the Catholic Church.

The Empress gave Paul the secluded estate of Gatchina in 1783, and there the Czarevitch established his own small court. His passion for military parade began to show itself, as he endeavored in every way to Prussianize his regiments. Catherine succeeded in alienating Paul from Maria Feodorovna, so that he turned to mistresses. He became thereafter increasingly morose and violent, fancying that he detected a revolutionary spirit in everybody and everything. One of the Czarevitch's most faithful friends said of him at this period: "Paul intends to rule with a rod of iron, and he is already putting his ideas into practice." [6]

The Jesuits Are Apprehensive

When Paul ascended the throne in 1796, Napoleon was amazing Europe by his first military triumphs. The new Emperor of Russia was a man forty-two years of age, deeply embittered and with a tragically warped mind. He had long felt that his mother was usurping a throne rightfully his. However, Paul I began with a noble proclamation of general peace. He freed Kosciuszko and all the other Poles imprisoned in St. Petersburg, and he restricted the labor which a serf had to do for his squire. Paul was less benign to the gentry. He reduced their importance, and enhanced that of the agents of his bureaucracy.

The Jesuits in White Russia did not know what to expect. Would the capricious sovereign turn against them because his mother had protected them? In May, 1797, Emperor Paul visited the Jesuit college in Orsha, together with the Empress and two of their sons, Alexander and Constantine. Paul was most gracious and on leaving the college, he said to the Jesuits, "I have always greatly esteemed your Society, and I still esteem it." [7]

To others among his subjects, however, Paul was the reverse of gracious. He forced a tight Prussian uniform and detested Prussian drill on the Russian troops. At almost every military drill some officers were victims of the Emperor's sudden anger, and not a few of them were abruptly sent to Siberia. The despot recalled Russians who were traveling in Western Europe, banned French books and music, and forbade costumes suggestive of revolutionary Paris.

Paul governed by means of ukases, issued at random and dealing alike with the most important affairs of the Empire and the pettiest questions of private life. The smallest infractions of an ukase brought swift punishment, and the number of person exiled or imprisoned by Paul was enormous. The ruler's continual interference in the private lives of his subjects aroused their exasperated hatred.

Protector of Catholic Cardinals

The revolutionary French had expelled Pius VI from Rome, and turned the Eternal City into a republic. In 1798 the indignant Emperor Paul decided to join Austria and England in their war against France. Suvorov won astounding victories over the French in Italy, but the Austrians became uncomfortable about this Russian warrior of genius. They arranged to have the Russian general march into a rattrap in Switzerland. The peerless Suvorov, trusting "in God and the wonderful devotion of his men," eventually saved his troops from capture.

Embittered by the selfishness of his allies, Paul withdrew his army. The despot turned against Suvorov, because he discovered that the aged warrior had ignored some niggling imperial military regulations. The exhausted hero died a few days after his arrival in St. Petersburg, and Paul could not prevent his subjects from observing the day of Suvorov's funeral as one of national mourning.

Pope Pius VI died in a prison in France on August 27, 1799. In September Cardinal Rezzonico arrived in St. Petersburg. He had been sent by the College of Cardinals to ask the protection of Emperor Paul for the bereaved Catholic Church, and the Russian ruler received this request graciously. The cardinals met in conclave in Venice, under the protection of Emperor Paul of Russia and Emperor Francis of Austria. After three and a half months Cardinal Chiarmonti was elected Pope and took the name of Pius VII.[8]

The Pope Recognizes the Jesuits

The secret society of the Illuminati had been founded in Bavaria in 1776. At this time it had numerous lodges in St. Petersburg and it had acquired a strong hold on the Russian nobility. Emperor Paul learned of the antisocial and antimonarchic tendencies of the Illuminati, and read a book which recommended the activities of the Jesuits, especially their education of youth, as the best antidote against the perverse doctrines of the secret society. On the spot, Paul desired to open Jesuit colleges all over Russia. But Father Gruber told the Emperor that the Society of Jesus in Russia would have to receive public papal recognition before this could be done.

On August 11, 1800, Paul accordingly wrote to Pius VII, making a formal request for the Pope's public recognition of the Jesuits. Unfortunately, the Catholic prelate whom Emperor Paul sent to Rome with this letter did not arrive at the Papal Court until January, 1801. Pius VII received with joy the Emperor's request. On March 7, 1801, the Pope signed the brief recognizing the legal existence of the Society of Jesus in Russia. Then the Holy Father wrote to Paul I, thanking the Russian sovereign for his signal services to the Catholic Church. But before the arrival of the Pope's letter in Russia, Paul had been murdered.[9]

Jesuits in the Russian Capital

While the Russian Emperor was awaiting word from Pius VII, he entrusted the Catholic Church of St. Catherine in St. Petersburg to the care of the Jesuits. Paul had discovered the continual scheming of Archbishop Siestrzencewicz against the

Society of Jesus. The Emperor took the St. Petersburg residence of this unworthy prelate for a Jesuit school, then he exiled Archbishop Siestrzencewicz to his country estate and placed him under police surveillance.

The foreign Catholics of St. Petersburg were quickly won by the zeal of their new pastors. Orthodox nobles and merchants frequented the Catholic services and attended in considerable numbers the catechetical lectures given by the Fathers in the afternoons. The Russian aristocracy begged Father Gruber to open a boarding school for their children in the capital, and this was done in 1802.

Under Paul I the Uniates enjoyed a blessed interval of toleration. Revolutionary France had ceased to protect Catholic missions in the Orient, and the Russian Emperor planned to take these abandoned missions under his care. Seeing the Emperor's predilection for the Jesuits, the Patriarch of Constantinople himself begged that Jesuit missioners might be sent to the islands of the Greek Archipelago.

Violent Death of Paul I

After Napoleon had seized supreme power in France under the title of First Consul, he treated for peace and even for alliance with Russia. Paul then saw in the First Consul his ally in the crusade for altar and throne. In order to co-operate with Napoleon, Paul placed an embargo on all English ships, thus cutting off the increasingly important hemp trade of the Russian landowners with Britain.

But now a conspiracy against the Emperor was coming to a head. Paul's mad suspicions were a danger to his own family, so Alexander agreed to the deposition of his parent. The heir to the throne did, indeed, make the condition that his father's life should be spared, but this did not save Paul's eldest son from experiencing bitter remorse during the rest of his days.

On the night of March 23, 1801, the conspirators entered

the Emperor's bedroom and demanded his abdication. A struggle ensued, in the course of which the sovereign was knocked down and strangled with an officer's scarf. At the time of his assassination, Paul was meditating a project of union of the Churches. "By order of the Emperor, the Orthodox bishops were sharpening their pens," says Father Pierling.[10]

Footnotes to Chapter Ten

[1] Stanislas Zalenski, *Les Jésuites de la Russie-Blanche*. Vol. I, pp. 240–63.
[2] Paul Pierling, *La Russie et le Saint-Siège*. Vol. V, pp. 124–58.
[3] Stanislas Zalenski, *op. cit.* Vol. I, pp. 410–22.
[4] Paul Pierling, *op. cit.* Vol. V, pp. 173–76.
[5] Catherine II, *Letter to Grimm,* in K. Waliszewski's *The Romance of an Empress,* p. 251.
[6] Henry Smith Williams, *The Historians' History of the World*. Vol. XVII, p. 414.
[7] Paul Pierling, *op. cit.* Vol. V, pp. 292–95.
[8] *Ibid.,* pp. 297–300.
[9] Stanislas Zalenski, *op. cit.* Vol. II, pp. 83–102.
[10] Paul Pierling, *op. cit.* Vol. V, pp. 309–27.

CHAPTER ELEVEN

The Northern Sphinx

THE NAPOLEONIC epic and the heroic patriotism of the embattled Russian people lend grandeur to the reign of Alexander I. Against this vivid background of bravery, glory, and gore the handsome figure of Catherine's grandson assumes the pleasing but shifting outlines of a fluid enigma. Napoleon himself was deceived by the baffling charm of the Russian Emperor, and at St. Helena he spoke of Alexander as "the Northern Sphinx."

Alexander's "liberal" teachers imparted no definite religious beliefs to the gentle and dreamy imperial child. Later, he would say to a Swedish Lutheran friend who was thinking of entering the Orthodox Church: "Personally, I don't care what a man's religion is, because all the Churches are good." [1]

Alexander had to observe an entirely different etiquette at his grandmother's splendid palace and at Paul's pedantic little military court at Gatchina. He learned early to dissimulate and remained throughout his life a consummate actor. In 1793, when Alexander was sixteen years of age, his grandmother arranged for her darling a marriage with a beautiful princess of Baden, who was renamed Elizabeth Alexeivna in the Orthodox Church. Alexander did not long remain faithful to his young wife. The children of the unhappy marriage, two daughters, died in infancy.

On his accession to the throne Alexander made peace with England. Together with four young liberal friends he formed a Private Committee, which met daily to plan the regeneration of Russia. In this initial period of his reign Alexander did more than any previous ruler to promote schools and universities in the Empire. Generally speaking, however, very little was accomplished by the Private Committee.

In the autumn of 1801 Russia annexed Georgia. After the annexation all Georgians were declared members of the Russian Church and only the Russian liturgy was allowed. Thus the ancient, independent Georgian Church ceased to exist. Owing to the labors of devoted Catholic apostles, there were Uniates in Georgia. Before many years had passed, the Georgian Uniates were obliged to flee into more tolerant Turkey or, if they remained, were forced into Russian schism.[2]

"Tender Solicitude" for Catholics

Alexander assured Pius VII that he would have "a tender solicitude for the Catholics in his Empire." The new Emperor did not intend to champion the Society of Jesus to the extent that his father had done. Archbishop Siestrzencewicz was recalled to St. Petersburg and placed at the head of an ecclesiastical college (bureau) for the government of the Catholics in Russia. The members of this college were ordered to govern according to the laws and the rules of the Catholic Church, but at the same time to conform to the imperial ukases. Rome did not fail to appreciate the grave dangers of this anticanonical institution.

Emperor Alexander did not deliver the Pope's brief of restoration to the Jesuits until September, 1802. At the same time the Fathers were reminded that they were to undertake nothing that might prove harmful to the "dominant religion." Any proselytism would result in the withdrawal of imperial protection from the Order, and even in the expulsion of the Jesuits from Russia.[3]

Father Gruber was elected General of the Jesuits in October, 1802. The following year Count Joseph de Maistre arrived in St. Petersburg as the ambassador of Sardinia. This brilliant Frenchman and ardent Catholic became very friendly with both Emperor Alexander and the Jesuits. In that same year the Emperor asked the Jesuits to open missions along the Volga River, and in the city of Riga. In 1804 the Government sent the Fathers to Odessa, and in 1805, to Astrakhan. In 1811 Jesuit missioners were requested by Alexander for apostolic work in Siberia.

Along the Volga River and at Odessa the mission work of the Jesuits was among German Catholic colonists. At Riga the Fathers brought numerous Letts back to a knowledge of their Catholic faith. At Astrakhan the Jesuits' parishioners were Catholic Armenian merchants. The Fathers also evangelized the neighboring Kalmucks, and extended their apostolate to the Caucasus, where they ministered to Poles enrolled in the Russian army and to Polish political prisoners. Then the spiritual needs of Polish exiles took the Jesuits to far Siberia.

In the spring of 1805 a fire broke out in the Jesuit residence in St. Petersburg. For some months Father Gruber had not been well, but he insisted on helping to extinguish the flames. The ailing General was so exhausted that he died shortly afterwards. All the nobility of St. Petersburg attended the funeral of the great Jesuit.[4]

Bitter Experiences of Archbishop Arezzo

A papal envoy, Archbishop Tommaso Arezzo, arrived in St. Petersburg in April, 1803. He had no contact with the Emperor beyond official audiences. The envoy was concerned about state control of Catholic seminaries. In December, 1803, a law was enacted forbidding all Russian Catholics to correspond directly with the Holy See, and the penalties for the breaking of this law were of the utmost severity.

Alexander I protected the Uniates during his reign and their numbers increased. But Archbishop Arezzo was suspicious of a ruling by which the Uniates were entitled to appeal directly to the Russian Senate. The fears of the papal envoy were justified. The Uniates were later granted their own separate ecclesiastical college, which soon became dependent upon the Orthodox Synod.

In June, 1804, Archbishop Arezzo was curtly dismissed from Russia, because Alexander's pride had been offended by a political incident in Rome. The papal envoy summarized his bitter experience in St. Petersburg as follows: "It is better to be a sacristan in Rome than an ambassador in Russia." After the Russian dismissal of the papal representative successive laws tightened the state control of the Catholic Church in the Empire.[5]

Imperial Duel

Alexander could not brook the successes of the "upstart French Emperor," so he formed against Napoleon a coalition of Russia, England, Austria, Sweden, Naples, and Prussia. Napoleon defeated this coalition in December, 1805, and the subsequent peace put an end to the old Holy Roman Empire. Fighting was resumed in 1806, with Napoleon on one side and Russia and Prussia on the other. Again the French Emperor defeated his enemies. Then Napoleon offered to meet personally with Alexander.

The two sovereigns met in 1807 at Tilsit on a raft on the Niemen River. The plan proposed by Napoleon was that he should have a free hand in Western Europe, and Alexander in the East. Prussia's share of Poland was made into the independent Grand Duchy of Warsaw, under the protection of France. In Russia the alliance of Napoleon and Alexander was highly unpopular, but the latter was merely biding his time. In 1808 Alexander annexed Finland. Four years later Russia took Bessarabia from Turkey, and obtained recognition of her protectorate over the Christian population among the Turks.

In 1811 the nobility of White Russia asked Alexander to make the Jesuit college in Polotsk a university. At that time both Alexander and Napoleon were endeavoring to win the adherence of the Poles, and Alexander knew that he would please the Catholic population of White Russia by sanctioning a Jesuit university at Polotsk. He did so, and the university began to function in January, 1813.[6]

Napoleon's Fatal Blunder

Meanwhile the semblance of friendship between Napoleon and Alexander was wearing thin. Napoleon gradually massed on the Russian frontier a huge army of Frenchmen and subject peoples. On June 23, 1812, he crossed the Niemen River and entered the vast domains of Alexander. The Russian Emperor took an oath that he would not make peace until the last French soldier had left the soil of the Fatherland.[7]

Napoleon found himself irresolute in this strange, immense country. The Russian generals would not come to grips with him, and many of his own troops deserted into the great, empty plains. The French entered Moscow, but of a sudden the ancient capital of the Czars began to burn. Alexander did not seek peace. There was nothing left but to retreat. Harassed by the Russian generals and terrorized by the swift attacks of Cossacks and partisan bands, the Grand Army froze and starved to death in the desolate emptiness. Napoleon abandoned the remnants of his troops and returned to France.

During the struggle between Napoleon and Alexander the

French soldiers pillaged, damaged, and sometimes even burned the Jesuit establishments in White Russia. Because of the thousands of unburied corpses of combatants, there was an epidemic at Polotsk. Over thirty-three Jesuits in White Russia died during the years 1812 and 1813.

Liberator of Europe

In January, 1813, Alexander led his troops across the frontier in order to liberate Europe from the tyranny of Napoleon. Alexander was reaping the prestige of a victory won primarily by the heroism of the Russian masses. In October, 1813, the allies broke up Napoleon's new army at Leipzig, and the following spring, the Russian Emperor made a glorious entrance into Paris. He showed himself magnanimous to Napoleon, obtaining for his defeated rival the sovereignty of the little island of Elba. Pope Pius VII had been imprisoned by Napoleon at Fontainebleau. On his return to Rome, the Pontiff promulgated the brief of world restoration of the Society of Jesus. In Russia Archbishop Siestrzencewicz and the secret societies were disquieted by the triumph of the Jesuits.

In the Congress of Vienna (1815) the victorious allies quarreled among themselves, but the scare of Napoleon's return from Elba reunited them. The Russian Army was too far off to take a part in the final defeat of Napoleon at Waterloo. Alexander's reaction to the strain of the recent war years took the form of a vague but exalted mysticism. It was in this frame of mind that he proposed his scheme for a Holy Alliance of Sovereigns. The rulers of Russia, Prussia, Austria, France, Spain, Naples, and Sardinia joined the Holy Alliance. Alexander was vexed with Pius VII for refusing to sign its charter. But the Pope was right. As time passed, the Holy Alliance helped to cloak with mysticism a general policy of repression.[8]

Enemies of the Jesuits Prevail

While Alexander was crusading in Europe, storm clouds were gathering over the heads of the Jesuits in St. Petersburg. The Russian Minister of Cults, Prince Galitzin, became their relentless enemy when one of his nephews, a pupil in the Jesuit boarding school, became a Catholic. It was furthermore rumored that some ladies of the court had embraced Catholicism, owing to the influence of the Fathers.

On his return from Western Europe Alexander found the nobility of his capital agog about the Jesuits and their converts. The enemies of the Society had no difficulty in convincing the Emperor that he should expel the Jesuits from Russia. The expulsion of the Fathers from St. Petersburg was the preliminary step. It took place in December, 1815.[9]

At the Congress of Vienna the bulk of the Duchy of Warsaw had been given to Alexander. He loyally fulfilled his promise to grant Poland a constitution, and he emancipated the serfs in Estonia, Kurland, and Livonia. But in Russia proper the Emperor furthered the foundation of military colonies, hated by the peasants. The whole population of these military villages was put under a rigorous drill and supervision. In education, too, a period of reaction set in. Under the influence of Metternich, the reactionary Minister of Austria, Alexander opposed all popular movements for liberation in Europe. Alexander's brother, the Grand Duke Constantine, was viceroy in Poland and his regime was one of harsh oppression.

In the spring of 1820 the election of a new General of the Jesuits was to take place in Rome. Prince Galitzin thereupon pointed out to Alexander the danger of having in Russia a Society with headquarters in a foreign country. The sovereign forthwith issued an ukase expelling the Jesuits from the whole Empire. The expulsion took place during Holy Week. Everywhere the faithful said farewell to the Fathers with tears and followed them for long distances out of the towns. As the Russian Government had difficulty in replacing the Jesuits in the Caucasus, it kept two of the Fathers in those arduous mission outposts until 1826.[10]

The "Blessed of God" Dies

With the years the mystical tendencies of Alexander deepened, but in his mysticism, as in all else, the Emperor was unstable and restless. In 1825, shortly before his death, the Emperor sent General Michaud de Beauretour on a personal mission to Pope Leo XII. The nature of this mission has remained a secret. Alexander drew closer to his wife in the final years of his life. He accompanied the ailing Empress Elizabeth to Taganrog on the Sea of Azov, and surrounded her with affectionate attentions. On a visit to the Crimea the Emperor contracted a severe chill which led to gastric fever. Alexander Pavlovitch died in December, 1825.

The Catholic Church in Russia had not fared well under the gentle Czar. By his tightening of state control and by his expulsion of the Jesuits, the "Blessed of God," as the Orthodox called Alexander I, had wrought incalculable harm to Catholicism in his Empire. But when Alexander expelled the sons of Saint Ignatius, their Society had been restored in the whole world, and Russia had played to the full her providential role of preserver of the Jesuits.[11]

Footnotes to Chapter Eleven

[1] Nicolas Brian-Chaninov, *L'Eglise Russe,* p. 173.

[2] Adrian Fortescue, *The Orthodox Eastern Church,* pp. 17 f., 304 f.

[3] Paul Pierling, *La Russie et le Saint-Siège.* Vol. V, pp. 338–43.

[4] Stanislas Zalenski, *Les Jésuites de la Russie-Blanche.* Vol. II, pp. 116–44.

[5] Paul Pierling, *op. cit.* Vol. V, pp. 350–448.

[6] Stanislas Zalenski, *op. cit.* Vol. II, pp. 160–65.

[7] Nicholas Mikhailovitch, Grand Duke of Russia, *L'Empereur Alexandre Ier*. Vol. I, p. 97.
[8] *Ibid*. Vol. II, pp. 210–14.
[9] Stanislas Zalenski, *op. cit*. Vol. II, pp. 213–43.
[10] *Ibid.*, pp. 245–63.
[11] Adrien Boudou, *Le Saint-Siège et la Russie*. Vol. I, pp. 131–39.

CHAPTER TWELVE

"Conversion" by the Knout

NICHOLAS I, the successor of his elder brother, Alexander, was born in 1796, the year of the death of Catherine the Great. In 1817 the young prince married the daughter of Frederick William III of Prussia, who was rechristened in the Orthodox Church as Alexandra Feodorovna. The marriage proved happy and fruitful. The reign of Nicholas I had a somber beginning. On December 26, 1825, two thousand soldiers of the Guard, stirred up by officers who were members of secret societies, attempted an insurrection.

The "Decembrist" leaders belonged to the Russian aristocracy and with the suppression of their insurrection, the leading role in the nation fell to the bureaucracy. But the ideas of the Decembrists survived their abortive revolution. Five of the conspirators were hanged, and the other principal revolutionists were exiled to Siberia. One of the prominent Decembrists, Michael Lunin, was a Catholic, baptized during a sojourn in France. Condemned to twenty years of hard labor in Siberia, Lunin left a diary which reveals his Christlike acceptance of his bitter lot.[1]

A Despot by Conviction

In the early years of his reign Nicholas I fought successfully against Persia and Turkey, winning additional Armenian provinces and a privileged position on the Black Sea and in the Straits. The new Emperor was an imposing and coldly handsome man, six feet three inches tall. He had an iron will and a passion for military minutiae, but he was honest and full of a sense of duty. Nicholas had no use for liberal ideas. He was proud of his role as secular head of the national Church, and he considered it as both a religious and a political duty to restore the Catholic Uniates to the bosom of the Russian State Church.

The political police were organized in this reign to a point where the Russian citizen no longer had any private life, and Nicholas forbade his subjects to travel abroad. Yet this autocrat by conviction attempted a number of reforms on behalf of the serfs. Nicholas established as High Procurator in the Court of the Holy Synod, Protasov, a general of the hussars, who had no scruples about dragooning the Uniates of White Russia and Lithuania.

In this stifling atmosphere the national Church was not without spiritual glories. Seraphim of Sarov, the last Russian saint canonized by the Orthodox Church, was teaching his "way to the acquisition of the Holy Ghost." The Optyna Monastery in the midst of thick forests of the Kaluga region was rebuilt at this time and grew into a large community. At Optyna famous monks became spiritual directors of men of the world.[2]

The Road of Truth

The Russians of high birth who had become Catholics in the time of Alexander I were obliged to live abroad during the reign of Nicholas in order to escape legal penalties. Madame

Sophia Svetchin opened a famous salon in Paris; Father Ivan Gagarin, S.J., and Father Ivan Martynov, S.J., founded the Slavonic Library in the French capital; and their pupil, Father Paul Pierling, S.J., later wrote authoritative books on the history of the Catholic Church in Russia.[3]

The Catholic Russian émigrés made no great impression on Russian society, but Peter Chaadaiev did. This aristocrat was profoundly influenced by the writings of French Catholic thinkers. In 1836 Chaadaiev's *Philosophical Letters* caused a sensation. Chaadaiev said that as a consequence of the Eastern Schism Russia had been cut off from the stream of universal Christianity and her spiritual and cultural life had stagnated. To the reproaches of his countrymen Chaadaiev replied, "It is not by the road of the Fatherland, but by the road of truth, that we ascend to heaven." Nicholas I declared Chaadaiev insane and had him placed under medical supervision. In spite of his profoundly Catholic ideas, Peter Chaadaiev died in the Orthodox communion.[4]

Plight of the Uniates

In 1827 Joseph Siemashko, the son of a Uniate priest of the Ukraine, submitted to the Emperor a plan for the reunion of the Ruthenian Uniates with the Russian State Church. Nicholas welcomed with joy a helper in the very bosom of the Church which he wished to suppress. The traitor was raised to the episcopate and made a suffragan of Metropolitan Bulhak, a faithful Catholic.

Another Polish rising took place in 1830 with an attempt to kill the hated Viceroy Constantine, the brother of the Russian Emperor. Warsaw capitulated the following year, and Poland was made a mere province of Russia. The Polish insurrection found many of its most zealous partisans among the Ruthenian Uniates, so Nicholas I was all the more determined to insure their loyalty to Russia by reuniting them with the Russian State Church.

The number of Uniate bishoprics was reduced to two, and an ukase of 1832 decreed that all sons born of marriages between Catholic and Orthodox Christians would belong to the Russian State Church. Two other traitorous Uniate priests were raised to the episcopate. In 1837 the Uniate ecclesiastical college in St. Petersburg was made subject to the Holy Synod of the State Church. The faithful Metropolitan Bulhak died the following year, and the Emperor lowered himself by having the deceased prelate buried as a member of the schismatic Church.

At Polotsk in 1839 Siemashko and his two renegade companions in the Ruthenian Uniate episcopate induced over thirteen hundred Uniate priests to request reunion with the State Church of Russia. Nicholas I made haste to sanction the reunion, saying, "I thank God and I authorize it." By this act of violence 1,600,000 Ruthenian Uniates were forcibly incorporated into the Russian State Church.

Many of the Ruthenian laity and six hundred Uniate priests refused to submit to the "reunion" of Polotsk. The Russian Government then resorted to open force. The "recalcitrant" priests were degraded and imprisoned in remote monasteries. The prisons, the knout, and Siberia made thousands of martyrs of the laity. In reward for his services Bishop Siemashko was appointed metropolitan. He organized missions to win over to schism the "stubborn" Uniates.[5]

After 1839 the Ruthenian Uniate Church in Russia remained alive only in the Chelm diocese, in Russian Poland. This district had been ceded by Austria in 1815, and was less severely dealt with. At Chelm the Ruthenian Uniate Church lingered on for a few decades longer, until it, too, succumbed to the wiles of a traitorous Uniate prelate.

Catholics of the Latin Rite

The timeserving Archbishop Siestrzencewicz died in 1826. His successors were mostly compliant men, who did not dare to protest governmental infringements on the rights of the Church. In 1842 the Emperor arbitrarily transferred the central seminary for Latin Catholics from Vilna to St. Petersburg.

In December, 1845, Nicholas I made two personal visits to Pope Gregory XVI. The Pontiff requested that the Catholics in Russia be permitted uncensored correspondence with the Holy See. This the Emperor would not grant. On the other hand the Pope refused to give his blessing to the central Catholic seminary founded by the Emperor in such an irregular manner in St. Petersburg. Nicholas I was not offended by the Pope's forthrightness, and two years later he concluded an agreement with his successor, Pius IX.

As a result of the agreement between Pope Pius IX and the Russian ruler, it became possible to appoint bishops of the Latin rite to sees which had long been vacant. Property was restored to the Church, and a lay official was no longer to spy on the meetings of the Catholic prelates. In 1848 Pius IX arranged with Emperor Nicholas that all the Catholics of the Caucasus should be placed under the jurisdiction of the Roman Catholic Bishop of Tiraspol, a city fifty-five miles northwest of Odessa.[6]

A Striking Paradox

It is one of the striking paradoxes of Russian history that the birth and development of a rich literary culture occurred during the oppressive rule of Nicholas I. The brilliant young poets, Pushkin and Lermontov, died early in duels. The gifted literary critic, Vissarion Belinsky, founded a school of thought in Russia. Krylov wrote his mordant fables. Gogol fearlessly satirized bureaucratic abuses, and Ivan Turgenev was jailed for having powerfully depicted the evils of serfdom.

After the publication of Peter Chaadaiev's writings, Russian political thought became divided between the Westernizers and the Slavophiles. The Westernizers followed Chaadaiev in the belief that Western Europe was the home of vital progress, whereas the Slavophiles thought that the proud Westerners had much to learn from the patient poverty of the "God-bearing" Russian masses.

In the reign of Nicholas I, Glinka founded Russian national music. During those same years, an extraordinary young nobleman, Michael Bakunin, was the father of Russian anarchism. Banished to Siberia, he escaped and fled to America. From America Bakunin made his way to Western Europe, where he engaged in an epic struggle against Karl Marx.

A Proud Heart Breaks

Toward the close of his reign Nicholas I exiled to Siberia the young epileptic Dostoevsky, who was later to become one of the world's greatest writers. In 1853 the Emperor again made war on Turkey. The following year France and England entered the conflict on the side of Turkey, and the allies decided to emphasize their initial successes by an invasion of the Crimea. In the ensuing siege of Sevastopol the common soldiers of Russia manifested their customary heroism, but there was as yet no railway system south of Moscow in the Empire, and supplies failed to reach the troops.

Nicholas saw his vaunted system crumbling about him. The "iron Emperor" was broken and his proud heart bled. In the midst of his mental excitement he contracted a fatal chill. The Autocrat of All the Russias died as a devout Orthodox Christian on March 2, 1855. The European predominance of St. Petersburg, built up by Catherine II and enlarged by Alexander I, was no more.

During the Crimean War religious persecution broke out with fresh violence in Russia. In retaliation for Turkey's measures against her Orthodox subjects Nicholas organized a formidable persecution of all subjects of the Russian Empire who did not belong to the State Church. "Obstinate" Ruthenian Uniates were again flogged, jailed, or sent to Siberia.[7]

Footnotes to Chapter Twelve

[1] Helen Iswolsky, *Soul of Russia,* pp. 116 f.
[2] G. P. Fedotov, editor, *A Treasury of Russian Spirituality,* pp. 242–79.
[3] Serge Bolshakoff, *Russian Nonconformity,* pp. 146 f.
[4] Gregor Alexinsky, *Russia and Europe,* pp. 249–57.
[5] Adrien Boudou, *Le Saint-Siège et la Russie.* Vol. I, pp. 153–231.
[6] Leopold Braun, *Mission Studies,* September, 1950, "The Faith and the Peoples of Russia," pp. 65 f.
[7] *Ibid.,* p. 59.

CHAPTER THIRTEEN

"Catholicism Means Revolution!"

ALEXANDER II was thirty-seven years of age when he ascended the throne of Russia, during the course of the Crimean War and under the most difficult circumstances. As Czarevitch he had married Princess Wilhelmina Marie of Hesse-Darmstadt, and over the years she bore him six sons and two daughters. There was not in this tolerant and compassionate man the making of a soldier Czar. In religion, Alexander II was in no sense a mystic or a fanatic. He believed in doing good and in submitting himself humbly to the will of God.

The Crimean War ended in 1856. Extremists in Russia were dissatisfied with the Treaty of Paris, but the new Emperor said the peace was worth the terms which had to be given for it. Alexander II granted a general amnesty to Polish prisoners and restored the Catholic bishoprics in Poland. He nevertheless warned the Poles that they must give up dreaming of independence.

In Russia itself Alexander gave permission for travel abroad and abolished the restrictions by which his father had hampered the universities. Before long the new generation of students began to assume an active part in politics, important reviews blossomed, and newspapers were founded. The sudden flowering of national self-expression gave birth to superb Russian literature and music, but it also let loose destructive forces.

Pope Pius IX sent Archbishop Chigi to attend the coronation of Alexander II (1856). The Emperor granted an audience to the Pope's representative, in the course of which the new sovereign made it clear that he intended to follow his father's policies in regard to the Catholic Church.[1]

Serfdom Abolished

The reform that preoccupied Alexander II the most was the abolition of serfdom. At his accession about one third of the population were serfs. Committees of the gentry for the study of projects of emancipation were set up in every province. A committee to draft the actual laws was established in 1859. At length, in March, 1861, the emancipating edict was read out in all the churches of the Empire.

The serfs were on the whole disappointed. They felt that they should possess all the land they cultivated, but after the emancipation the village commune had only half of the former squire's estate. Consequently, the reform of 1861 seemed abortive to the peasants and they dreamed of completing it. This dream was a cause of the Russian Revolution of 1917.

As delays blocked the progress of emancipation, the new Russian radicals, dubbed by Ivan Turgenev "Nihilists," demanded more drastic measures. Fly sheets began to appear calling for terrorist acts against the government and even for the murder of the Emperor. It was discovered that the Russian revolutionary leaders were abetting disorders in Poland.

Persecution in Poland and Lithuania

On October 15, 1861, the anniversary of Kosciuszko's death, the Poles flocked into the churches of Warsaw, singing the forbidden patriotic hymns. Russian troops then forced their way into the churches, drove out the Poles, and arrested their prominent leaders. Archbishop Felinski of Warsaw protested against the violent invasion of the sacred edifices. He was therefore arrested, tried by court-martial, and sent into exile.

The planned insurrection, begun early in 1863, was put down within a few weeks' time. The Russian court-martials showed no mercy to priest or layman guilty of rebellion. In Lithuania the brutal General Muraviev declared that it was "useless to make prisoners." Public opinion in Russia was aroused by the Poles' claim to Lithuania. Even the liberals felt that the Poles must be Russianized at all costs. The last vestiges of Polish autonomy were suppressed, and the Russian language was made obligatory in all the educational institutions of Poland. Catholic nobles were commanded to leave the country and to sell their estates, which only schismatics were permitted to purchase.

The Catholic Church in Poland suffered in a special manner, as the supposed fomenter of the rising. The seminaries were placed under the control of the civil authorities, and numerous monasteries were suppressed. Many of the clergy were sent to Siberia where they were treated as ordinary criminals. Those who remained were subjected to the supervision of the police. In Lithuania General Muraviev forbade the use of the Polish language. He ordered hundreds of Catholic churches to be closed under the pretext that they had been Orthodox four centuries previously. Pius IX protested fearlessly against the sufferings of Catholics in Poland and Lithuania.[2]

In an audience granted him by the Holy Father in December, 1866, the Russian chargé d'affaires, Baron Felix Meyendorff, declared that the Catholics were everywhere the accomplices of the rebels. "Catholicism means revolution!" he exclaimed. Pius IX thereupon abruptly dismissed Baron Meyendorff from his presence. The Russian embassy to the

Vatican was consequently at once recalled, and an imperial ukase was issued abrogating all the conventions between Russia and the Holy See.[3]

From then on the lot of the Latin Catholics and of the Ruthenian Uniates in Poland was even harder. At this time the Catholic prelate of Mogilev, Maximilian Staniewski, a Dominican, was so misguided as to co-operate with the plans of the government for making the Catholic Church a state institution. On his death-bed, in 1871, this disloyal prelate repented of his conduct and begged that it might not be imitated.

Fertile New Life

In these years railways were developed and private banks were founded. From the middle of the nineteenth century to the beginning of the twentieth, the population of the Empire doubled. Alexander II was more tolerant in dealing with the Jews than any other Czar before or since. Two new universities were founded, that of Odessa and that of Warsaw. Trial by jury was introduced into the law courts. Conscription was declared to be an equal obligation for all the classes, and the whole system of army training and education was reorganized. From then on it was in the army that most Russian peasants learned how to read and write.

In 1864 district and provincial *Zemstvos* (county councils) were established. These new authorities of local self-government were elective and many of the best men in the country were glad to enter this patriotic service. Largely because of the *Zemstvos* education and medical care spread far and wide in Russia, reaching even the peasant huts.

As the reforms of Alexander II went into effect, all Russia became conscious of new life. Journalism flourished. The masterpieces of Ivan Turgenev, Fyodor Dostoevsky, and Leo Tolstoy gave splendor to Russian literature. Russian music entered into a period of creative activity, illuminated by the genius of Balakirev, Mussorgsky, Borodin, Rimsky-Korsakov, and Tchaikovsky. Russian scientists began to prove themselves capable of the technological inventions of the modern age.

New life also surged through the national Church. Orthodoxy emphasized the idea of *sobornost* (congregationalism), stressing that the faithful as a whole, clergy and laity, should participate in the affairs of the Church. The Russian State Church continued to produce outstanding monks known as *startzi* (elders), who exercised a great influence upon all classes of society. Dostoevsky developed the idea that it is not the Church which should resemble the State, but the State which should be transformed into the Church and thus ascend to become a Church over the whole world. "This is the glorious destiny ordained for the Orthodox Church. This star will arise in the East!" [4]

Revolutionists and Reaction

In the reign of Alexander II Turkestan and the khanates of Bukhara and Khiva fell under Russian domination. The Russians were approaching the frontiers of India, and England took alarm. China ceded to Russia the whole left bank of the Amur and a great tract on the right bank which reached to the Pacific at Vladivostok. Russia secured from Japan the whole of Sakhalin Island in return for the Kuril Islands. Russian imperialism thus manifested itself by a marked advance in Asia. A desire to reach an understanding with the United States was one of the basic reasons for Russia's sale of Alaska to our country (1867).

On April 14, 1866, a young student fired at Alexander II and missed his aim. From that time the government lived in suspicion of the students. Reaction set in, especially in the fields of education and of the press. Switzerland and England became refuges for Russian revolutionists. The first volume of

Marx's *Capital* was translated into Russian in 1872, but the tenets of Marxism did not immediately make any wide appeal in the Empire.[5]

The more moderate of the radical students, the propagandists, thought that the whole world could be changed by education and persuasion. Hundreds of them settled down in the peasant villages, especially as schoolteachers. But the peasants themselves did not know what to make of their new helpers. The failure of propaganda methods made more and more of the students insurrectionists, and the insurrectionists tended increasingly to terrorism.

Suppression of the Uniates of Chelm

The forcible "reconversion" of the 250,000 Uniates in the Chelm diocese had been proceeding since 1866. The stanch Bishop Jan Kalinski was sent to Siberia and replaced by Canon Wojcicki, who worked in sympathy with the Russian Government. Pope Pius IX excommunicated Wojcicki in 1867. Four years later Canon Marcel Popiel, a traitorous Uniate priest, was named Administrator. Faithful clergy were deported and replaced by Russian Orthodox priests from Galicia. In 1875 the see of Chelm was suppressed, and the Russian Government announced that its Ruthenian Catholics had voluntarily passed over to Orthodoxy. Such was far from being the case.[6]

Ruthenian Uniate peasants who refused to accept the schismatic priests forced upon them were flogged with the cruel Cossack whip. The Cossacks received orders to "hunt down" the faithful Uniates and to destroy their crops. The Emperor created a new Orthodox diocese of Lublin and appointed Popiel its bishop, but the peasant "converts" declined to enter the Russian churches. Austria remained the last refuge of the Ruthenian Uniates.

New Diplomatic Rupture

In 1877 the Russo-Turkish War made it useful for the Empire to conciliate its Catholics. Prince Leo Urusov, the Russian chargé d'affaires in Rome, presented to the Holy See the outlines of a plan for settling all the religious questions pending between the two governments. Cardinal Simeoni, the Pontifical Secretary of State, thereupon gave to the Russian representative a statement of grievances and demands.

After a delay of two weeks, this paper, instead of being forwarded to St. Petersburg, was insultingly returned. Prince Urusov was consequently summarily dismissed from the Papal Court. This new rupture of diplomatic relations did not improve the sad condition of Catholics in Russia.[7]

War and Terrorism

Turkey was making no attempt to respect the religious liberty of her Christian subjects. The Russian people were thoroughly aroused by the Turkish oppression of their coreligionists, and public opinion forced the Emperor to declare war on Turkey in 1877. By the spring of 1878 the defeated Turks were eager for peace and signed a treaty with Russia. But then, under threat of war, the nations of Western Europe demanded that the gains of Russia be minimized. Alexander had to contend with the enmity of the powerful Bismarck in the newly established German Empire in addition to the jealous hostility of England.

The forcible revision of Russia's treaty with the Turks by the Western European Powers cost Alexander II the greater part of his popularity in Russia. In the general disappointment demands arose on all sides for a Russian parliament, and the revolutionary movement made marked headway. High officials were murdered, while constant attempts were made on the life of the Emperor himself.

Statesmanship of Leo XIII

When Leo XIII was elected Pope in 1878, he sought a renewal of relations with Russia. In a personal letter to Alexander II, written in 1880, the Pope asked the Emperor to protect the Catholic Church in his Empire. "Your Majesty cannot be ignorant of the fact that the Catholic religion deems it her duty everywhere to spread the spirit of peace and to labor to preserve the tranquillity of kingdoms and peoples," said Leo XIII.

The Pope's words made an impression on Alexander II. Before the close of the year, the Emperor sent to Rome two of his sons, Sergius and Paul. The two Grand Dukes were instrumental in renewing friendly intercourse between the Vatican and St. Petersburg. But the prospect of a firm religious peace for Catholics in Russia was suddenly and rudely dispelled by the tragic death of the Emperor.[8]

A Monstrous Crime

On March 13, 1881, Alexander II signed a constitutional manifesto, a plan for accommodating a representative system with the autocracy. He then drove out to attend to his daily duties. A young Nihilist threw a bomb at his carriage. The Emperor got out to speak to some Cossacks of his suite who had been wounded. At that moment a second assassin hurled a bomb between Alexander's feet.

Alexander II passed away unconscious an hour and a half later. The revolutionists had slain one of the kindest and the most humane of monarchs, and the bomb that killed the Czar of Freedom put an end to the faint beginnings of Russian constitutionalism.

Footnotes to Chapter Thirteen

[1] Adrien Boudou, *Le Saint-Siège et la Russie*. Vol. II, pp. 60 f.
[2] *Ibid.*, pp. 217–32.
[3] John R. G. Hassard, *A Life of Pope Pius IX,* p. 163.
[4] Fyodor Dostoevsky, *The Brothers Karamazov,* p. 66.
[5] Stephen Graham, *Tsar of Freedom: The Life and Reign of Alexander II,* pp. 104 f.
[6] John Gilmary Shea, *The Life of Pope Pius IX,* pp. 399–401.
[7] James MacCaffrey, *History of the Catholic Church in the Nineteenth Century*. Vol. I, p. 402.
[8] Bernard O'Reilly, *Life of Leo XIII,* pp. 373 f.

CHAPTER FOURTEEN

Patience of Leo XIII with Russia

TENSION BETWEEN the Vatican and St. Petersburg lessened during the reign of Alexander III (1881–1894), simply because Alexander and his ministers could not resist the masterful, warmly courteous diplomacy of Pope Leo XIII. At the beginning of his pontificate Leo XIII was inspired by a radiant vision of the Eastern Church tending toward union with the Holy See, and this great hope made him nobly patient with Russia until the end of his long life.

Alexander Alexandrovitch, a blond giant with a light beard, was laborious, innately honest, and loved the simple pleasures of home and family. Although he was extremely limited in his outlook, he had the instinct and the tact of a statesman. His Empress was the former Princess Dagmar of Denmark, who was received into the Orthodox Church with the name of Marie Feodorovna. The chief adviser of Alexander III was his former tutor, a ruthless authoritarian of considerable intellectual brilliance. The new Emperor made this Constantine Pobiedonostev Procurator of the Holy Synod.

Alexander III had the five leading conspirators against his

father's life hanged. The rest of the terrorists were imprisoned or sent to Siberia. The revolutionary organizations were virtually destroyed. Moreover, public opinion had turned against the terrorists. The accession manifesto of the new ruler contained the words "with faith in the power and the right of autocracy."

A Meager Agreement

The murder of Alexander II had horrified Leo XIII. The Pope wrote to Alexander III, saying that he had no greater desire than to co-operate with the Emperor in spreading Christian principles in Russia, and asking that his efforts might have Alexander's support and protection. In his Encyclical, *Diuturnum,* Leo XIII warned all governments and peoples that the chief cause of the current social disorders lay in their having abandoned Christ's teaching on civil societies and civil duties and virtues.

On March 30, 1881, two envoys of the Russian Government arrived in Rome to resume the negotiations begun in the last years of the reign of Alexander II. After long and difficult discussions, a meager agreement between the Vatican and the Russian Government was reached in December, 1882. The vacant sees in Russia and in Poland were to be filled, and the Catholic seminaries were to be restored, to some extent at least, to the control of their bishops. In the consistory of March 15, 1883, Leo XIII had the happiness of preconizing twelve new prelates for Russia.

It proved impossible to obtain any measures in favor of the "reconverted" Ruthenian Uniates in the diocese of Chelm. The Vatican was dryly informed that Russia considered these Christians as members of the Orthodox Church, and that for political reasons this attitude could not be modified.[1]

Archbishop Vannutelli in Russia

On the occasion of the coronation of Alexander III in May, 1883, Leo XIII sent as ambassador to Russia Archbishop Vincent Vannutelli, a prelate of exceptional tact and distinction. He was received with marked cordiality by the Emperor, who praised the services which the Pope was rendering to social order. Alexander III said that a permanent official representative of Russia at the Vatican would be appointed, but this promise was not fulfilled until 1894, the last year of Alexander's reign.

The stay of Archbishop Vannutelli in Russia proper affords a rare and revealing view of the attitude of the Russian Orthodox masses toward the Catholic religion. They manifested great reverence to the envoy of the "Pope of Rome." In large numbers they gathered in the streets to receive the Latin prelate's blessing, crossing themselves meanwhile devoutly after the Eastern manner.

Catholics in Russia and in the Polish provinces assembled at the railway stations, and waited long hours to receive the blessing of the Pope's envoy. In one town a weeping Uniate woman broke through the cordon of soldiers and threw herself at the Archbishop's feet, crying out: "It is now twelve years since we have been able to receive the sacraments. Help us!" [2]

Apostle of Union

At Moscow, Archbishop Vannutelli met Vladimir Soloviev, a young Russian inspired by the ideas of Yury Krijanitch and Peter Chaadaiev. As a result of his profound study of the New Testament and of Church History, Soloviev reached the conclusion that the Roman Papacy was truly appointed by Christ to represent Him on earth. He believed that the historical mission and destiny of Russia is to provide the Catholic Church with the political power which is needed to save Europe and the world. Such were the basic ideas of Soloviev's *Russia and the Universal Church,* published at Paris in 1888 in order to escape the Russian censorship.

Following the lead of Krijanitch, Soloviev objected to the adoption of the Latin rite by Russian Catholics and to their denationalization. In 1896 Father Nicholas Tolstoy, a Catholic priest of the Eastern rite, received Soloviev into the Catholic Church. The influence of Vladimir Soloviev has been great among his compatriots. Today, thinking Russians still eagerly seek his writings, though they can be found only with difficulty under the Soviet regime.[3]

Program of Reaction

The political program of Alexander III for his Empire was extremely simple. It consisted in opposing all liberal and revolutionary movements, and in satisfying to a certain extent the urgent economic needs of the Russian people. In 1890 the Land Captains were established, officials chosen from the poorer gentry whose function was to supervise every detail of peasant life. The peasants saw in them a partial revival of serfdom.

The press was stifled during this entire period, and the law courts fell increasingly under governmental control. All autonomy was taken from the universities, but the government of Alexander III promoted technical schools of all kinds. Children of the lower classes were excluded from the secondary schools.

Pobiedonostev was the very soul of this program of reaction. In the Orthodox Church the sermons of preachers were subject to ecclesiastical censorship. Village priests were ordered to report to the police those of their parishioners who were "politically untrustworthy." Every form of religious dissent was severely penalized.

A systematic endeavor was made to spread among the various peoples of the Empire the language, religion, and administrative institutions of the dominant race. Orthodox missioners were said to win back yearly to the State Church between eight and ten thousand Old Believers. But after freedom of conscience was proclaimed early in the twentieth century, these "conversions" ceased.[4]

Of all the various races the Jews were the most severely treated. They were heavily handicapped in education and professional advancement. Pobiedonostev is reported to have predicted that his policy would drive one third of the Jews to starvation, one third to emigration, and the remaining third to conversion.

No Diplomatic Rupture

In the midst of all this intensive Russianization of the many peoples of the Empire, it is not surprising that the agreement of 1882 between the Holy See and St. Petersburg was not always observed by the Russian officials. Imperial orders were never discarded, no matter how unimportant they might be. The accumulation of these orders constituted a series of precedents, dignified by the name of "fundamental laws of the Empire," which tied in red tape the hands even of rulers and of officials of good will.

Catholic priests and prelates continued to be exiled. The civil authorities still interfered in the seminaries and in the parishes. Churches were arbitrarily closed or handed over to the state religion. But there was no rupture of diplomatic relations. A Pope who viewed earthly happenings in the light of the "eternal philosophy" of Saint Thomas Aquinas could afford to be patient with Russia.[5]

Social Developments

The peasants occupied more and more land in Russia proper, and the more ambitious among them ventured forth to Siberia, continuing the process which peopled the Russian Empire. Their eastward migration was facilitated by the construction of the Trans-Siberian Railway, begun in 1892. Numerous peasants moved to some great town, especially to St. Petersburg or to Moscow, and became factory workers.

Russia was becoming an industrial nation. Vast deposits of coal and iron were found in southern Russia on the Donets River, and workers flocked from all sides to this region. The new industrialists were as crude as the new workers. Because of pressure from the employers, the government increasingly disregarded the welfare of the workers. By this time Marx's *Capital* was the most widely read book among Russian students, but it was still practically unknown to the general public.

During the eleven years which followed 1892 Russia had a remarkable Minister of Finance, Count Sergius Witte. He established a gold standard and accumulated a large gold reserve, thus enabling Russia to win financial confidence in Western countries and to attract foreign capital. Witte's policy received firm support from Alexander III, who was invariably careful with the national economy.

The name of Social Democrats, already in use in Germany, began to be applied to the Russian Marxists in about 1893. Isolated acts of terrorism took place. In 1887 Alexander Ulianov, the son of a district school inspector in the Volga town of Simbirsk, was hanged for having conspired against the life of the Emperor. Thirty years later Alexander's seventeen-year-old brother, Vladimir Ulianov (Lenin), was to be the main architect of the social upheaval that replaced the autocracy of the Romanovs with the dictatorship of the Soviets.

The prevailing tendency in this reign, however, was not socialism, but liberalism. The *Zemstvos* performed notable educational and medical services, and advised the peasants how to make the best use of their holdings. In marked contrast with the fine, unselfish work of the *Zemstvos,* bureaucratic corruption was again rife during the reign of Alexander III.

Russia Represented at the Vatican

In his foreign policy Alexander III became increasingly suspicious of Bismarck's hostile designs. In 1894 he therefore ratified a military convention with France. As the danger of a clash between Russia and Germany grew imminent, Pope Leo XIII said that he might be prepared to use his influence with the Poles in a direction favorable to the Czarist Government. In 1888, Russia accordingly sent to Rome a promising young diplomat, Alexander Petrovitch Iswolsky. Leo XIII then gave instructions to the Polish bishops that they were to "impress upon the faithful the duty of obedience to the secular power and of docility towards the ruling authorities."

In 1893 of its own accord, the Russian Government entrusted the Armenian Uniates to the care of the Latin bishop of Tiraspol. At that time a Catholic seminary was founded in Tiflis. The following year Alexander III at length appointed Alexander Iswolsky his permanent official representative at the Vatican.[6]

Accession of the Last Romanov Emperor

In the autumn of 1894 the great strength of Alexander III had been sapped by an incurable malady. He died on November 1, having received Holy Communion from Father John of Kronstadt, considered by the Orthodox a living saint and a thaumaturge.

The new Emperor was, like his father, a devout member of the Orthodox Church. Nicholas II was a fatalist who remained wrapped in an enigmatic and inert calm. His will was hopelessly weak and he was constantly under someone's influence, until he finally became completely dominated by his wife, Empress Alexandra Feodorovna, the former Princess Alix of Hesse-Darmstadt.

Nicholas II declared for an "unswerving adherence to the principle of autocracy." This pronouncement of the new sovereign was taken as a direct challenge by the revolutionists and they intensified their activity. Already a strong Marxist movement had grown up in Russia. Now a Social Revolutionary Party was formed, quite distinct from the Social Democrats. The Social Revolutionists labored among the peasantry, and they quickly won their support by proclaiming that all the land should belong to the peasants.

At his coronation Nicholas II was exhausted by the weight of his crown and robes. Symbolically, the heavy scepter fell from his weak grasp. The new Emperor continued his father's unifying policy of Russianization, and forcible conversion of his Moslem subjects was attempted. The Jews suffered especially in this reign. As a result of the territorial acquisitions of Peter the Great and his successors about half of the Jews in the world were then subjects of the Russian Emperor.[7]

In 1898 the Russian Minister of War learned that Austria was improving her artillery at a time when Russia was not in a position to follow her example. Count Witte suggested an initiative for a general stopping of armaments, and this idea was adopted by Nicholas II in his invitation to a Conference of the Powers at The Hague. At the Conference detailed proposals for limiting the horrors of war were agreed upon, and a permanent court of arbitration was set up.

Concessions to Catholics

The Russian alliance with France and the increasing influence of Austria in the Balkans made it desirable for Nicholas II to preserve good relations with the Papacy. He was disposed to make certain concessions to Catholics, but his efforts were often defeated by hostile officials. The unbending Pobiedonostev, in particular, was Procurator of the Holy Synod until 1905. In 1898 the Emperor permitted certain religious orders to reside in Poland, and the following year he allowed Catholic priests to visit Rome. In 1902 Nicholas sent a Councilor of State to represent him at the celebration of the Golden Jubilee of Leo XIII.

Wishing to prove its good will the Russian Government offered to assign to the Catholic Armenians the separate bishopric which had been promised to them since 1847. This bishopric was accordingly established with its see at Tiflis. Today about seventy thousand Armenian Catholics in Russia are isolated by the Soviet regime from the Catholic world.

In May, 1904, the zealous Catholic prelate of Mogilev, Archbishop George Szembek, called a sort of synod of all the Latin Catholic bishops in the Empire. He sought to ascertain their chief desires and needs, in view of a memorial to be presented to Nicholas II. The greater part of the desires then expressed by the Catholic hierarchy in Russia were satisfied by the edict of tolerance in April, 1905.[8]

Footnotes to Chapter Fourteen

[1] Adrien Boudou, *Le Saint-Siège et la Russie.* Vol. II, pp. 530–40.
[2] *Ibid.,* pp. 542–45.
[3] Helen Iswolsky, *Soul of Russia,* pp. 154–56.
[4] Kenneth Scott Latourette, *A History of the Expansion of Christianity.* Vol. IV, p. 129.
[5] Adrien Boudou, *op. cit.* Vol. II, pp. 549 f.
[6] James MacCaffrey, *History of the Catholic Church in the Nineteenth Century.* Vol. I, p. 403.
[7] N. S. Timasheff, *Religion in Soviet Russia,* p. 4.
[8] A. M. Ammann, *Storia della Chiesa Russa,* pp. 505–10.

CHAPTER FIFTEEN

Grudging Liberty to Catholics

THE FIRST period of the reign of Nicholas II was a time of comparative domestic quiet, but political unrest was growing. In 1902 the Minister of the Interior was murdered by terrorists, and was succeeded by the reactionary Plehve. The Emperor had taken a dislike to Witte, because the latter opposed the policy of aggression in the Far East; so in 1903 Count Witte was abruptly deprived of the Ministry of Finance. Plehve now had a free hand and he authorized armed attacks upon the Jews. He also urged a "small, victorious war," as a sure means of averting impending revolution.

In those years the encroachments of Russia in Manchuria and in Korea had made war with Japan inevitable. To the amazement of the world the Japanese were victorious on land and sea in 1905. Plehve did not live to see the disastrous outcome of his "small, victorious war," because he was assassinated in the summer of 1904. At that time was born at last a male heir to the Russian throne, but it was soon discovered that the child was subject to the haemophilic tendency inherent in his mother's family. This meant that the Czarevitch

Alexis might at any time bleed to death from a slight cut or wound.

After the fall of Port Arthur indignation against the government rose to white heat in Russia. Strikes broke out everywhere, and the whole country was placed under police authority. The Emperor's uncle, the despotic Grand Duke Sergius, was blown to pieces by a bomb on February 17, 1905. Faithful friends of the Emperor begged him to rally the loyal elements of the public by reasonable concessions before it was too late.

Edict of Toleration

On April 30, 1905, Nicholas accordingly decreed religious toleration in Russia. He was congratulated by Pope Pius X. The Emperor repealed the statutes which forbade members of the Orthodox Church to join other denominations, but propaganda was still forbidden to the non-Orthodox faiths. Within two years after the edict of toleration had been issued in Russia, five hundred thousand persons embraced Catholicism. Catholics of the Byzantine rite were still illegal, so the returning Ruthenian Uniates had to embrace the Latin form of Catholicism.[1]

Already at the end of the nineteenth century a few courageous Orthodox priests, influenced by the ideas of Vladimir Soloviev, had become Catholics, but they did not wish to adhere to the Latin rite. In 1908 the broadminded Prime Minister, P. A. Stolypin, authorized in St. Petersburg a small chapel for Russian Catholics of the Byzantine-Slav rite. A little community of Russian Catholics of the Eastern rite in Moscow sought in vain recognition by the State. In 1910 Pius X entrusted the Russian Catholic priests of the Byzantine-Slav rite to the supervision of the greathearted Ruthenian Uniate Metropolitan in Galicia, Archbishop Andrew Shepticky.[2]

The Imperial Duma

In August, 1905, Nicholas II most unwillingly instituted a national assembly, the Imperial Duma. But the public was not satisfied, because the franchise was arbitrarily restricted and the Duma was only to be consultative. Open criticism and disorder continued all over the Empire. The Socialist parties set up a Soviet, or council of elected delegates, which at once took the lead in the workers' movement. In October the Emperor promised a wide extension of franchise for the Duma and gave it a legislative character. The Soviet nevertheless fomented numerous strikes, but the general public had turned against them. By December the abortive revolution of 1905 had virtually run its course.

The First Duma, elected in the spring of 1906, was soon in flat opposition with the government. It was brusquely dissolved in July. During the elections for the Second Duma a large number of revolutionists were voted in. By this time the Social Democrats were divided into two sections: the Bolsheviks (extremists), under Lenin; and the Mensheviks (moderates), who were followers of George Plekhanov. Before long the Second Duma was also summarily dissolved, and thirty-one of its Social Democrats were exiled to Siberia.

When the Third Duma met in November, 1907, *Zemstvo* members and professional men had a majority of seats. The Third Duma lived out its full term of five years and gained universal respect. The Fourth Duma, elected in 1912, was composed of practically the same personnel as the Third. It was still in session at the outbreak of the March Revolution in 1917.

Catholics Hampered by Police Regulations

Ever since 1905 the Russian bureaucrats had made it their business to invent technical excuses for taking away the liberties supposedly granted to Catholics by the State. Archbishop Kluczynski of Mogilev was so persecuted by police ordinances that in 1914 he obtained permission to resign his see. It remained vacant until after the abdication of Nicholas II.

The Russian Government was especially hostile to Russian Catholics of the Byzantine-Slav rite, because it perceived in this movement a real danger to the State Church. A few Catholic priests of this rite were found "guilty of proselytism" and expelled from Russia. The Catholic chapel of the Byzantine-Slav rite in St. Petersburg was closed on the grounds that "the church building did not fulfill the technical conditions obligatory to buildings where public meetings are held." [3]

Last Cultural Glories

On June 28, 1914, the assassination in Sarajevo of Archduke Francis Ferdinand, the heir to the Austrian throne, ignited Europe's explosive rivalries. In the ensuing Armageddon of World War I the Russia of the Czars was to perish. A backward glance over the reign of Nicholas II shows that the last cultural glories of the Czarist regime were not unworthy of its long history. The character of the instruction in Russian universities at this time cannot be considered inferior to that of the universities of Western Europe during the same period. The Russian intelligentsia was second to none in the world, but the Empire as a whole had an illiteracy figure of well over sixty per cent. It could not claim a broad popular culture.

A new school of Russian painters designed superb stage settings. Skriabin, Rachmaninov, and Stravinsky convinced the world anew that Russia is among the most musically gifted of nations. In international scientific circles, the names of Mendeleiev, Pavlov, and Popov acquired high prestige.

Anton Chekhov, Maxim Gorky, and Leonid Andreyev cannot be regarded as the equals of Turgenev, Tolstoy, and

Dostoevsky, but they nevertheless rank high among novelists and playwrights. In the beginning of the twentieth century Russian poetry was dominated by the Symbolist movement, deeply influenced by the mystical writings of Vladimir Soloviev. Later, one of the Symbolist poets, Vyacheslav Ivanov, could not endure the Bolshevist assault on Christianity. He escaped from Russia and became a Catholic of the Byzantine-Slav rite.[4]

In 1903 a number of Russian writers and professional men became the sponsors of a "religious-philosophical movement," which followed the ideas of Dostoevsky and emphasized the messianic mission of Russia. They have exercised a powerful influence on modern Orthodox thought. One member of this group, Nicholas Berdyaev (1874–1948) became internationally known. Though not hostile to Rome, he had no desire for reunion.

After the Bolshevist Revolution Berdyaev affirmed that the triumphs of Communism are due to the fact that Christianity has not put its truth into full, living practice. "It is no use opposing Communism with ideas; it can only be done with religious realities. Communism is false, not because exalted ideas govern history, but because God exists as a tremendous reality, and strength and the last word belong to Him," wrote Berdyaev.[5]

On the brink of World War I the Russian Empire covered almost a sixth of the surface of the globe, with a population estimated at 180,000,000. Millions of needy peasants envied and hated the two hundred thousand landlords who still owned about a quarter of the arable land in European Russia. The restless two and a half million industrial workers were denied legal means of expression. The Czarist policy of discrimination against non-Russian nationalities made it certain that these numerous peoples of the Empire would not stand by the throne in the event of revolution.

Metropolitan Shepticky

In the beginning Russian public opinion was enthusiastically for the war, and the German name of the Russian capital was soon changed to Petrograd. Russia won initial victories over the Austrians in Galicia. During their precarious occupation of Galicia the Russians attempted forcible "conversion" of the Ruthenian Uniates of that region. The great churchman, Andrew Shepticky, Uniate Metropolitan of Lwow, was interned by the Russians for eighteen months and was liberated only after the Emperor's abdication.

A significant event occurred during Metropolitan Shepticky's captivity. He was sent to the monastic prison of Suzdal in Russia proper, and was lodged in a highly unhealthy hermitage where several Orthodox monks had died in rapid succession. The local villagers speculated as to how long the "heretical" prelate would survive the rigors of this death-trap. The peasants soon heard very favorable reports about this kindly stranger. When Metropolitan Shepticky was still hale and hearty after the lapse of a month, the peasants decided he was a saint. They declared themselves of his religion, whatever it might be! The alarmed authorities hastily dispatched the Uniate prelate to Yaroslav.[6]

Regime of Rasputin

By the end of August, 1915, the ill-equipped and ill-fed Russian troops had been pushed out of Russian Poland. Public clamor arose against the inept failures of the Czarist Government, and a Progressive Bloc formed in the Duma. It seemed as if Russia were at last about to have a constitution. But the Empress Alexandra Feodorovna desired above all things that her son should receive his autocratic inheritance intact, and the weak Nicholas was putty in the hands of his wife. The

Empress, in turn, had fallen completely under the influence of Gregory Rasputin, a coarse Siberian peasant.

Possessed of hypnotic healing powers, Rasputin had been of great aid in nearly fatal crises in the bleeding malady of the Czarevitch Alexis. The Siberian peasant was heartily opposed to the war. He told the Empress to persuade Nicholas II to take over in person the supreme military command. After the Emperor had left for Headquarters at the front, Rasputin became the real ruler of the rear. Sordid political and financial intrigues flourished, and the morale of the noncombatants was breaking down. On December 30, 1916, Rasputin was assassinated, but the harm had been done. People spoke openly of replacing Nicholas II by his son, with a regent.

The March Revolution

At Petrograd, in February, 1917, there was a stoppage of the food supply, attributed by the public to the incompetence of the government. On March 8 crowds milled around the baker's shops, and the following day police fired on them. From then on disorders mounted. On March 11 the Duma appointed a Provisional Committee, but the Social Democrats were unwilling to join it. That evening they held in the lobby of the Duma the first meeting of a Soviet hastily elected from the factories and barracks. The President of the Provisional Committee telegraphed to the Emperor, urging the immediate appointment of a Prime Minister who would have the confidence of the nation. Nicholas II did not answer.

On March 14, Ministers of the Provisional Government were appointed. Alexander Kerensky, who was a member of the Duma and also Vice-President of the Soviet, was offered the Ministry of Justice. The Soviet circulated among the troops at the front Army Order No. 1, the effect of which was to destroy the authority of the officers.

During the night of March 15 two delegates of the Provisional Government requested Nicholas II to abdicate. On account of the incurable ailment of his son, the Emperor abdicated in favor of his only brother, the Grand Duke Michael. Shortly afterwards "Colonel Nicholas" was placed under arrest. The Grand Duke Michael said that he would not ascend the throne, unless he should be asked to do so by the Constituent Assembly when it met. This decision (March 16) proved to be the end of the Russian monarchy, which had stood for over a thousand years and now had crumbled by its own insufficiency. There was nothing ready to take the place of its immense ruins.

Catholic Expansion

At the time of the abdication of Nicholas II some twelve million Catholics, mainly of Polish origin, resided within the confines of the Empire. There were a sufficient number of Catholic seminaries to ensure the perpetuity of the clergy. Russia counted three vast dioceses of the Latin rite. In addition to the Metropolitan See of Mogilev, there was the diocese of Kamenetz in Western Ukraine, and that of Tiraspol with its episcopal residence in Saratov on the Volga. Not a single city of importance in the Empire was without one or more Catholic churches.

But this expansion had taken place in spite of almost insurmountable obstacles, subtly elaborated by Czarist legislation. The confessions not legally recognized by the Czarist Government, such as the Ruthenian Uniates and the Catholics of the Byzantine-Slav rite, were treated worse. Both Latin Catholics and Uniates, therefore, hailed as a liberation the fall of the Czarist regime.[7]

Disorder Suits Lenin

The lack of direction in the March Revolution of 1917 suited admirably the purposes of a mastermind who was all too soon to replace the disorder by a uniform despotism, such as was never dreamed of by the most ruthless of the Czars. The steely mastermind was that of Lenin, the man who said: "Religion is the opiate of the people. . . . All contemporary religions, churches and all types of religious organizations, Marxism forever looks upon as organs of bourgeois reaction, serving to defend the exploitation and the stultifying of the working class." [8]

Footnotes to Chapter Fifteen

[1] Donald Attwater, *The Catholic Eastern Churches,* pp. 79 f.
[2] A. M. Ammann, *Storia della Chiesa Russa,* pp. 507–09.
[3] Maurice Baring, *The Mainsprings of Russia,* p. 139.
[4] Helen Iswolsky, *Soul of Russia,* pp. 162–74.
[5] Nicholas Berdyaev, "The Religion of Communism," in *Vital Realities,* publication of The Macmillan Company, pp. 149–89.
[6] Francis McCullagh, *The Bolshevik Persecution of Christianity,* p. 313.
[7] Leopold Braun, *Mission Studies,* September, 1950, "The Faith and the Peoples of Russia," pp. 69–73.
[8] Lenin, *Collected Works.* Tome XIV, p. 70.

CHAPTER SIXTEEN

"Religion is Like a Nail"

THE PROVISIONAL Government established universal suffrage for men and women throughout the land, and endeavored loyally to keep Russia in the war. It permitted the Orthodox Church to call a national council in Moscow. A Russian Patriarch was elected and provisions were made for a more vigorous parochial life, but these reforms came too late. Metropolitan Shepticky was freed and before he returned to Galicia, he held in Petrograd a synod for the Catholics of the Byzantine-Slav rite. According to the powers formerly granted to him by Pope Pius X, Metropolitan Shepticky appointed Monsignor Leonidas Feodorov his exarch for all Russia.

From the start the power of the Provisional Government was contested by the Soviet, which had close contact with the masses. Before long every town in Russia formed its Soviet, and similar organizations took place in the army and in many villages. On April 16, 1917, Lenin and his principal followers arrived in Petrograd from Switzerland. Lenin knew exactly how to appeal to the masses. His political platform consisted of four magic promises: "Peace, land, bread, power."

The Bolsheviks Take Over

The Bolsheviks rose unsuccessfully in May and again in July. After the July rising of the Bolsheviks Kerensky was appointed Prime Minister. The unstable condition of Petrograd made it urgent to transfer the ex-Emperor and his family to a place of safety, and Kerensky decided on Tobolsk in Siberia. Meanwhile, Kerensky was losing his grip on the helm of State, and the Bolsheviks took full advantage of his difficulties. On November 6, 1917, the revolutionary military committee established by the Bolsheviks in Petrograd decided to act.

By the following day the whole capital was in the hands of the Bolsheviks. Moscow was then taken and again made the capital of Russia. The victors formed a Government of People's Commissars with Lenin as Prime Minister and Trotsky at the Foreign Office. The Bolshevist leaders secured to the Communist Party a monopoly of political power and of publicity by abolition of the ballot and by terrorizing all opponents.

The factories were at once handed over to the "toilers," and production soon fell to one sixth. Private trade was abolished by decree. This led speedily to starvation in the towns. Banks were abolished, all land was declared to be national property, and the houses of the well-to-do were confiscated and became tenements crowded with workers' families.

Elections for the Constituent Assembly had begun all over Russia in November, 1917. But when it met, it did not give the Bolsheviks anything but a minority. Accordingly the Leninists dispersed the Constituent Assembly with machine guns on January 19, 1918. Two of the Assembly's most prominent members were murdered immediately afterwards.

On March 3, 1918, the Bolsheviks accepted German terms of peace, thereby sacrificing nearly all territory won by Russia since the accession of Peter the Great. In May, the Finns gained their independence from Russian domination. Civil war broke out in various parts of European Russia and Siberia. The insurgent forces were aided against the Reds by Allied troops, who made landings at Murmansk, Archangel, and Vladivostok.

The Communist leaders had the ex-Emperor, his wife, and his children transferred to Ekaterinburg in the Urals. There they were all brutally murdered in a cellar on July 16, 1918. That same summer the Grand Duke Michael and six other Romanovs were done to death in towns in the vicinity of Ekaterinburg.

The Red Terror rose to a furious tempo that autumn, after Lenin had been shot at by a Socialist Revolutionary. Wholesale massacres were conducted in the prisons, and local risings of peasants were savagely crushed. No one was safe from Bolshevist spies. More than a million Russians emigrated.

Anti-Religious Policy

The initial anti-religious policy of the Soviet Government had three main features: to deprive the churches of material means, legal existence, and their central organizations; to reduce the clergy to a status of social inferiority; and to undermine the influence of the churches on various phases of life, but more especially on education. Soviet law did not recognize church marriages. A marriage could be dissolved whenever one of the parties so desired.

The first Soviet Constitution guaranteed "the freedom of religious and anti-religious propaganda." But the churches were in no favorable position to carry on religious propaganda, whereas anti-religious propaganda was backed by the relentless drive of the Communist Party. In the Red Terror many Orthodox priests were slaughtered by mobs. In the confusion some Orthodox parishes followed their priests into other religious bodies. Thus, in Kharkov province, in 1918, Father

Potapii Emilianov went over to Catholicism, taking his whole flock of eight thousand souls with him.[1]

Concentrated Attack on Catholics

At first the Catholics in Russia welcomed the Soviet decree proclaiming the separation of Church and State, but they soon recognized it as merely a subterfuge serving to facilitate the savage effort to annihilate all religions. Time and time again, however, the Soviet Government was forced to admit the failure of its anti-religious assaults. Lunacharsky, the Soviet Commissar of Education, proclaimed wryly, "Religion is like a nail. The harder you hit it, the deeper it goes into the wood of the soul." [2]

After the Bolshevik Revolution the Catholic priests in Russia, most of whom were Poles, were obliged to become Soviet citizens. Archbishop Edward von Ropp of Mogilev was exiled, as was Father Zertchaninov of the Byzantine-Slav rite. In the diocese of Kamenetz a good third of the clergy was lost as early as 1918 as a result of the Bolshevist persecution. In the spring of 1919 Pope Benedict XV petitioned Lenin to order respect for the Russian clergy of all faiths. The Soviet Minister, Chicherin, replied to the Holy Father's plea with studied insolence.

Catholics in Georgia and the Armenian Catholics in the Caucasus were consistently persecuted by the Bolsheviks. By 1941 when the German *Wehrmacht* invaded Soviet Russia, the Armenian Catholic clergy had been entirely wiped out by starvation, imprisonment, or exile.

Famine and Economic Retreat

Civil war continued, but the Allied troops, discouraged by the weakness and confusion everywhere evident among the anti-Bolsheviks, withdrew from Russia. By November of 1920 the resistance of the insurgents was crushed. Meanwhile the ancient enemies of Russia, the Poles, advanced to Kiev, but they had to retreat before the charges of the Russian cavalry. In August, 1920, the Red Army advanced in turn to the very gates of Warsaw. But the Bolsheviks were routed at the last moment, and the Poles again invaded Russian territory. Lenin cut his losses by the Treaty of Riga (March, 1921). About ten million Ukrainians and White Russians thus passed under Polish rule.

By 1921 the policies of the Bolsheviks had ruined Russia. Then came a devastating drought and an epidemic of malaria. On the Volga, and later in the Ukraine and the Crimea, whole masses of the population wandered about in search of food and cases of cannibalism were reported. The American Relief Administration, led by Herbert Hoover, saved the lives of millions. Pope Pius XI sent a Papal Relief Mission to Russia to care for the needy without distinction of race, politics, or religion.[3]

Lenin realized that an economic retreat from Communism could no longer be deferred, so in March, 1921, he put through the New Economic Policy. The following spring Lenin had a stroke, and in January, 1924, the Red dictator died. Petrograd was renamed Leningrad in his honor; Lenin's tomb, built into the wall of the Kremlin, became the official shrine of a strange, new cult.

Frontal Attack on the Churches

A decree of February 26, 1922, ordered the surrender of all precious church articles under the pretext of aid to the famine victims. In May, when the Vatican proposed to buy the chalices and other sacred objects then being requisitioned from the Catholic churches in Petrograd, Rome received no reply from the Soviet Government. The bad faith of the Bolshevik leaders was evident.[4]

The Orthodox Patriarch Tikhon was imprisoned. Then some unworthy Orthodox clergy, stooges of the Soviet authorities, usurped the Patriarchal functions. They formed a heretical sect, The Living Church. One of the first acts of these renegades was to bring about the expulsion from Russia of Father Vladimir Abrikosov, a Catholic priest of the Byzantine-Slav rite who had opened a church in Moscow. Father Abrikosov's work in Moscow was continued by Exarch Leonidas Feodorov.

The firm attitude of England brought about the release from custody of Patriarch Tikhon in June, 1923. The Living Church had meanwhile split up into warring sects. The preceding year, when the Great Powers first met Bolshevik Russia in conference at Genoa, Pope Pius XI had urged the Allies to exact religious guarantees as an essential condition of recognition of Soviet Russia. This humane proposal was politely shelved.

Arrest By Night

The Catholic Archbishop John Cieplak, the successor of Archbishop von Ropp, had constant difficulties with the Soviet Government. On the night of March 2, 1923, all the Catholic priests in Petrograd, with the exception of a French Dominican, were arrested and ordered to appear before the Supreme Tribunal at Moscow.

The accusations made against the fifteen Catholic clergy had no legal basis, the three Soviet judges were bitterly hostile, there was no jury, and the defense was not permitted to summon any witnesses. The spectators of the trial were mostly rabid Communists, eager to see the accused receive the death penalty. The Prosecutor, Krylenko, sought to terrorize the accused by bitter sarcasm and bloodcurdling yelps.

A very interesting figure in the dock was the convert, Exarch Leonidas Feodorov, a Russian born in Petrograd and the grandson of a serf. Krylenko declared him to be the most dangerous of the accused, because of his unusual ability to attract Orthodox Christians to the Catholic Church and thus to form against the Proletarian Revolution the dreaded "united religious front." The Exarch spoke in court with great fervor and dignity. "If the Soviet Government orders me to act against my conscience, I do not obey," he said.[5]

The priests were accused of having conspired together to form a counterrevolutionary organization. The Red Procurator worked himself into a fury of anti-religious hatred and yelled at the prisoners: "Your religion, I spit on it, as I do on all religions!" On the last day of the trial, Archbishop Cieplak and Monsignor Budkiewicz were condemned to death, and the other priests were sentenced to prison terms of various lengths. The Archbishop's sentence was later commuted to ten years' imprisonment, but on Good Friday night Monsignor Budkiewicz was shot in the dark cellar of the headquarters of the secret police.

In November, 1923, the only Catholic seminary in Moscow was raided by the police. Its students had been working by day in Soviet factories or offices, and doing their studying secretly at night. During that same month the Dominican nuns of the Byzantine-Slav rite in Moscow were expelled from their convent. All the Catholic priests of the Eastern rite were in jail or in exile. By this time the hierarchy of the Latin Catholic Church in Russia and nearly all its senior priests had also been imprisoned or else driven out of the country.

Ridicule of Christianity

After the death of Lenin, Stalin, the "Man of Steel," undermined his rivals for power. This cunning son of a Georgian cobbler, who had once studied in an Orthodox seminary, held the key post of General Secretary of the Party. Supported throughout by the Party, Stalin overcame Lenin's former comrades and was supreme from 1928 onwards. The new direction was back to nationalism. Stalin proclaimed that he believed in the possibility of "Socialism in one country (Russia)."

Patriarch Tikhon died in 1925, and the government prevented the election of a new Patriarch. Successive acting Patriarchs were imprisoned. But in 1927 the last of these, Metropolitan Sergius of Nizhni-Novgorod, was able to make a compromise with the Communist Government and thus to retain his office. During these years the Soviet leaders engaged in systematic ridicule of Christianity. A publishing company called *The Atheist* was established, an anti-religious seminary was opened in Moscow, and anti-religious carnivals were celebrated at Christmas and Easter. In an effort to organize anti-religious activity the Militant Atheists' League was formed in February, 1925.

In its persecution of the Catholic Church during the years 1924 to 1928, the Soviet Government shot or imprisoned irreplaceable religious leaders. No ordinations to the Catholic priesthood were taking place in Russia, because the Bolsheviks had done away with the bishops. Pius XI established in Rome a special Russian Commission and sent one of its members to Russia to consecrate new bishops in secret. But the newly consecrated prelates were in their turn arrested by the Bolsheviks.[6]

"Cultural Strangulation" of the Churches

In 1928 Stalin embarked upon the First Five-Year Plan, which pounded along under fabulous difficulties. Workers were driven relentlessly, and "wreckers" of machinery were convicted by summary mass trials. A somber aspect of the First Five-Year Plan was Stalin's ruthless collectivization of agriculture. More than a million of the prosperous peasants (called *kulaks*) were liquidated in the process.

It became compulsory for teachers to introduce Communism into all their courses. Many eminent Russian scholars were at this time imprisoned, exiled, or executed, and the Academy of Sciences in Leningrad was remodelled on Communist lines.

In 1929 the Soviet Government renewed the direct attack on religion by closing hundreds of churches. A six-day week was introduced to make it difficult for workers to attend Mass on Sundays. The Soviet leaders now had recourse to "cultural strangulation" of the churches. Religious propaganda was no longer permitted, the new official slogan being "freedom of religious worship and of anti-religious propaganda." Faithful Christians could not advance in public life. In the schools "believing teachers" were dismissed.

The peasants on the collective farms refused to work if their churches were closed. Fearing a fresh famine, the Government yielded to their complaints. But the "cultural strangulation" policy was continued up to the years 1934–35.[7]

By now the Catholics in Russia were reduced to the conditions of the catacombs. In an encyclical of February 2, 1930, Pope Pius XI protested with special vigor against the corruption of the young in Russia. During that same year he decreed that the prayers recited by Catholic priests and faithful after Mass should be offered for Russia.

"On the Religious Front"

The Second Five-Year Plan was inaugurated in 1933. The threat of Hitler's Germany having become very real, Stalin could no longer afford to remain at variance with the Russian masses. He accordingly made a number of concessions to popular feeling, culminating with the publication of the draft of a new "democratic" Soviet Constitution in June, 1936.

During this period the Soviet Government also made small concessions "on the religious front." Frequent divorces were condemned. The disenfranchisement of priests and all other "non-workers" was abolished. The children of "non-workers" were allowed to enroll in all school grades.

In 1935 the deported Exarch Leonidas Feodorov died in the utmost want not far from Vyatka (now renamed Kirov). Since his death almost nothing is known concerning the Russian Catholics of the Eastern rite. Before the Revolution a total of over eight hundred priests ministered to Latin Catholics in the Russian Empire. By 1935 only forty-odd of those priests were still at liberty. Many of the arrested Catholic priests were laboring on vast public projects under the direction of police engineers and in the company of common-law bandits.[8]

On May 12, 1936, Pope Pius XI said in a public address: "The first peril, the greatest and the most general, is certainly Communism in all its forms, for it menaces everything openly or insidiously. . . . It attacks especially the Catholic religion and the Catholic Church."

In Russia, however, the Soviet Government was far from satisfied with its progress toward "militant atheism." Its attacks had brought about new understanding between the Orthodox and the Catholics. The Militant Atheists' League decayed for want of zeal. Children educated in anti-religious schools manifested an alarming belief in amulets and magic charms. Yaroslavsky, the leader of the Militant Atheists' League, lamented: "It is impossible to build up Communism in a society half of which believes in God and the other half fears the devil." [9]

Footnotes to Chapter Sixteen

[1] Francis McCullagh, *The Bolshevik Persecution of Christianity,* pp. 54 f.

[2] Bernard Pares, *Russia,* p. 172.

[3] A. M. Ammann, *Storia della Chiesa Russa,* p. 552.

[4] Edmund A. Walsh, *The Last Stand,* pp. 181–83.
[5] Francis McCullagh, *op. cit.,* pp. 135 f., 192.
[6] A. M. Ammann, *op. cit.,* p. 553.
[7] N. S. Timasheff, *Religion in Soviet Russia,* pp. 38–46.
[8] Leopold Braun, *Worldmission,* December, 1950, "Catholics Behind The Iron Curtain," p. 93.
[9] N. S. Timasheff, *op. cit.,* pp. 85–110.

CHAPTER SEVENTEEN

The Sword and the Spirit

THE NEW Soviet Constitution of 1936 affirmed again the separation of Church and State in the Soviet Union. But Soviet civil law requires that the clergy, in order to perform their ministry, must apply to the local lay authorities for registration. Thus the State always has the power to paralyze the activity of the clergy by refusing registration. Moreover, whenever it appears expedient to the Soviet authorities, the practice of religion becomes "counterrevolutionary propaganda," and as such is subject to criminal prosecution. The "neutral" Soviet State forbids believers to make converts, but it urges atheists to make aggressive use of anti-religious propaganda. Article 122 of the Soviet Penal Code makes it illegal for priests to give religious instruction to minors.[1]

The threat of attack by Germany and Japan caused Stalin to seek closer ties with the democracies. The Soviet dictator entered into diplomatic relations with the United States in 1933. President Franklin Roosevelt stipulated that United States citizens resident in the Soviet Union must enjoy religious liberty, and an American Assumptionist priest, Father Leopold Braun, was authorized to say Mass at the Church of St. Louis in Moscow. Stalin brought the Soviet Union into the League of Nations in 1934, but he became increasingly convinced of the League's weakness.

In Russia the years 1936, 1937, and 1938 witnessed a series of mass political trials and executions. Almost all the remaining original Bolshevist leaders were liquidated. The trials of prominent personages were only part of a vast purge of suspected "Trotskyites and traitors." Trotsky himself was murdered in Mexico in 1940, under highly suspicious circumstances.

Third Direct Attack on Religion

In 1936 Pius XI constituted Saint Thérèse of the Child Jesus Patron Saint of Russia. The following year appeared the Pope's masterly encyclical on Atheistic Communism, *Divini Redemptoris*. By 1936 there remained only one Catholic prelate in Moscow, the French Assumptionist, Bishop Neveu. Sickness forced him to leave the Soviet Union, and the Foreign Office promised him a return visa. It was never granted.

In 1937 acute, nation-wide religious persecution began for the third time in the Soviet Union. Nearly half of the population had courageously risked all in a subsequently suppressed census by stating that they still believed in God. Everywhere Orthodox clergy were arrested on fabricated charges of collaboration with Germany and Japan. By thus arresting priests, and by imposing crushing taxes on religious associations, the government was able to close many additional churches.[2]

During this same year Father Piotr Awglo, Catholic Administrator of Mogilev, died in the prison of that city. When the faithful went to claim his body, it was thrown out of the prison completely naked. Generally speaking, however, Catholicism had already been driven underground, so the main fury of this third full-scale attack on religion fell on the Orthodox clergy.

Expedient Halt of Persecution

Hitler's conquests in 1938 and 1939 so alarmed Stalin that he concluded a non-aggression pact with Germany in August, 1939. While the uneasy pact lasted, the Red Army invaded eastern Poland, Finland, the Baltic States, and Bessarabia. The new Pope, Pius XII, predicted that the approaching world conflict would exhaust the nations and leave them in a condition "of which the disruptive and revolutionary forces now holding themselves in readiness will not fail to take advantage, in the hope of striking a decisive blow at Christian Europe." [3]

In all the regions occupied by the Red Army Catholicism was relentlessly persecuted. In Galicia the conquerors permitted Metropolitan Shepticky to occupy his palace, but surrounded him with spies. Three weeks before the German invasion of Russia the Soviets deported to Siberia and Kazakstan more than thirty-four thousand Catholic Lithuanians, among whom were nearly a third of the Lithuanian Catholic clergy. In the territories incorporated outright by Russia during and after World War II there were some twelve million Catholics.

In 1939, influenced by dangerous international conditions and the urgent needs of internal unity, the Kremlin adopted in Russia proper a new religious policy, marked by expedient compromise. It was now proclaimed that Christianity had not always been a reactionary force in Russia. The closing of churches was halted, and the trials of clergy were stopped. In 1940 the seven-day week was restored and Sunday was made the day of rest. But at the same time huge sums were spent on the distribution of atheistic literature, and new emphasis was placed on atheistic teaching in the schools.

The Catholic Church in Russia had no share in the new "tolerance." By 1939 Soviet persecution had brought about its complete disorganization, and the number of Catholics in

Russia proper had dropped to about half a million. In 1941 the Catholic churches in the Soviet Union were forcibly closed. Only the Church of St. Louis in Moscow remained open, because it was protected by the 1933 agreement concluded with the United States.[4]

Hitler Invades Russia

In the early morning of June 22, 1941, Hitler repeated the fatal blunder of Napoleon by invading Russia. In August, 1941, Radio Moscow accused the German regime of menacing the very existence of Christianity. There was a cogent reason for Soviet insistence on Hitler's "paganism." During the early period of the war there existed in certain occupied regions of Russia a veritable fifth column. Among those who collaborated with the invaders were a number of Orthodox clergy, because the Germans promised to restore full liberty to the national Russian Church. This German propaganda was initially successful especially in the Ukraine.

The tide turned in the Russo-German struggle of World War II with the Soviet victory at Stalingrad on February 2, 1943. After Stalingrad the Soviet Armies surged westward, retaking the Russian land. The Soviet press complained that retreating German troops were pillaging and burning famous Orthodox churches and monasteries.

In May, 1943, Stalin "dissolved" the Third Communist International as a gesture of friendship to his democratic Allies. In reality the Comintern was never dissolved. It went underground while it was being groomed for more important tasks; in the postwar period, its leaders became the viceroys of the new Soviet Empire.

Soviet Plans for Orthodoxy

The Orthodox Church in unoccupied Russia loyally supported the war effort of the Soviet Government. Metropolitan

Sergius hailed Stalin as "the divinely appointed leader of our armed and cultural forces, guiding us to victory." In 1943 the Kremlin permitted the Orthodox Church to elect a Russian Patriarch, and the adulating Sergius was chosen for the office. The League of Militant Atheists was disbanded, and the newspaper, *The Atheist,* was suppressed. At the beginning of 1944 Orthodox seminaries were allowed to reopen in the principal Russian cities. Monasteries and numerous churches were returned to the Patriarchate. It was even accorded a printing press.

Readers of newspapers in the Western countries were inclined to hope that the Soviet Government had abandoned its fight against religion. They were deceived. At no time since 1917 had any of the fundamental anti-religious laws been revoked. Even in 1941, when Stalin had desperate need of Lend-Lease help, he did not yield to the friendly pressure of President Franklin Roosevelt, who urged him to increase the solidarity of the Allies by granting religious freedom in the Soviet Union.[5]

The truth of the matter was that the Soviet leaders had decided to make use of the Orthodox Church as a very expedient tool. The favor shown to it served to weld internal solidarity. Moreover, Stalin planned to exploit the new religious policy as a means of conciliating and attracting Orthodox populations in neighboring countries soon to become Soviet satellites. The Orthodox Church also provided the Soviet Government with a handy weapon to use in its attacks on the Vatican. In April, 1944, the Patriarch conveniently assailed the very principle of the Papacy.[6]

Patriarch Sergius died in 1944. His successor was Patriarch Alexis, a tall, majestic man, descended from a long line of aristocrats. By 1946 the number of Orthodox priests had risen to some thirty thousand from less than six thousand in 1939. The Patriarch was seen at important parades in the Red Square in the company of the highest Soviet officials.

Mounting Tension

After World War II the victorious Soviet Union ruthlessly subjected the peoples of the annexed and the satellite regions of Eastern Europe to the implacable yoke of totalitarian Communism. Sixty million Catholics were thus exposed to relentless persecution. In Asia the advance of Communist control threatened the Catholic missions on that huge continent.

Because Catholicism and Soviet Communism both claim the whole world as their field of action, the duel between the two must be to the death. As the Soviet Union embarked on its postwar career of expansion, it accordingly intensified its campaign of vilifying slander, insisting with monotonous fatuity that the Vatican supports all "Fascist" regimes.

The democracies vainly hoped that by manifesting a conciliatory attitude toward the Soviet Union they might win over their strange Ally to the support of a permanent world peace and to the respect of the rights of men and nations. But pacifism does not jibe with the belligerently messianic ideology of Soviet Communism. Tension mounted steadily between the Communist world and the "capitalistic West," a tension which began soon after Yalta and eventually became known as "the cold war."

Sovietized Third Rome Policies

The postwar Soviet Government favored and furthered every effort of the Russian Orthodox Church to establish its hegemony over all the other national Eastern Churches. This policy was a sovietized reversion to the old Russian dream of Moscow as the Third Rome. In July, 1948, a Pan-Orthodox Congress was held in Moscow. Orthodox leaders at the Moscow Congress discussed the most effective means of forcibly "converting" to Orthodoxy Catholics in the annexed and Soviet-satellite countries. At the same time the Kremlin carried out in the satellite countries persecutions designed to set up "national Catholic Churches," which would no longer recognize the supreme spiritual authority of the Pope.[7]

Many more thousands of Catholics in the Baltic States were either shot or deported to Soviet concentration camps, because they refused to apostatize. By now all the Lithuanian Catholic bishops are dead or in exile, and very few priests have survived the Soviet terror.

Soon after the return of the Red Army to Galicia in 1944, Metropolitan Andrew Shepticky died under suspicious circumstances, but the Russians permitted a solemn public funeral in honor of the revered prelate. The following Metropolitan, Joseph Slipy, was subsequently condemned to forced labor in a Soviet coal mine. In April, 1945, all the Uniate bishops and a large number of priests were jailed or deported. Then the Russians made use of three renegade Uniate priests, who humbly requested that the Ruthenian Catholic Uniates be permitted to enter the Russian Orthodox Church. The suppressed Ruthenian Church of Galicia ministered to 3,576,237 Catholics in 1940.

The eastern province of Czechoslovakia had been Subcarpathian Russia before World War I, and the majority of its Slavs were Catholic Uniates. Here, too, since 1945, the Soviet authorities have made use of every method to drive the population into the Russian Orthodox Church.

Persecution by Stooges

In the satellite countries Soviet Russia's Communist stooges have assiduously followed the lead of the Kremlin. Because of the centuries-long attachment of the Polish people to Catholicism, the Warsaw Government at first went slowly in exercising pressure to bring the Catholic Church in the nation under state control. But the tempo of persecution has accelerated surely and steadily.

In Albania about ten per cent of the population were Catholics. Within a few months after the Communists had seized power the organization of the Catholic Church in Albania had been completely destroyed and the clergy virtually wiped out. In October, 1948, the "conversion" of Rumania's Catholic Uniates to the Orthodox Church was officially celebrated. As for the Latin Catholics of Rumania, they have courageously resisted the determined efforts of the Communist officials to form a "national Catholic Church." There were only about forty thousand Catholics in Bulgaria. The Communist regime in that satellite nation therefore adopted a policy of slow strangulation.

In Yugoslavia Tito has manifested implacable hostility to the Catholic Church, an attitude that was not modified by his break with the Soviet Union. After the infamous trial and imprisonment of Aloysius Cardinal Stepinac (at the time Archbishop Stepinac), Catholic Primate of Yugoslavia, in 1946, the situation of the Catholic Church became steadily worse. Cardinal Stepinac is now confined to his native village of Krasic, and is not recognized as Catholic Primate by Tito's Government.

At the end of World War II Hungary's six million Catholics comprised over sixty-eight per cent of the population. After an initial period of caution the Hungarian Communists began in earnest to undermine the Catholic Church. The Hungarian Primate, Cardinal Mindszenty, vigorously protested the nationalization of all schools in 1948. The Cardinal was arrested, subjected to a trial of such depraved iniquity that global indignation was aroused, and sentenced to life imprisonment in February, 1949. In June, 1951, Archbishop Josef Groesz, successor to Cardinal Mindszentry as chairman of the Hungarian Board of Bishops, was likewise condemned to long imprisonment.

Seventy per cent of the population in Czechoslovakia was Catholic when the Communists seized power in February,

1948. The new Government founded a pro-Communist "Catholic Action." In March, 1951, the Communist officials banished the beloved Archbishop Beran from his see city of Prague. Four new "canons," either renegade clergy or police costumed as priests, were installed in the Prague cathedral.[8]

A Crucial Papal Decree

In the Soviet Union itself the Church of St. Louis in Moscow is the sole Catholic church still open. But in recent years the American Assumptionist priest in Moscow has been saying Mass in his private apartment, because he has not been allowed to hold any kind of religious service in the Church of St. Louis.

Pope Pius XII issued a decree, in July, 1949, which stated that all Catholics who freely professed the doctrine of atheistic Communism, and who defended and propagated that doctrine, were subject *ipso facto* to the special excommunication reserved to the Apostolic See, from which only the Pope himself could grant absolution. Answering a question of a representative of Reuters, Patriarch Alexis affirmed that the excommunication of supporters of Communism would fundamentally contradict the teaching of the Orthodox Church. He added that there could be no conflict for believers between loyalty to the Russian Orthodox Church and to the Soviet State.

The Vatican learned in 1950 that the Kremlin was training trusted Communist nationals of the satellite lands to pose as Catholic priests or monks in their own countries. These men were being prepared in two "seminaries" and ten special schools, directed by an apostate priest. The pace of the whole anti-religious campaign in the Soviet-satellite countries was noticeably intensified after the Communist Information Bureau (Cominform) held meetings in Poland and Hungary in 1949 and 1950.[9]

Pushkin and Lenin

The social structure of the Soviet Union survived World War II virtually unchanged. Millions still toil in the forced labor camps, and the higher government employees continue to have their "country houses," their expensive private cars, and the luxurious Blue Express to carry them south to their vacation resorts.

During the Russo-German struggle circumstances obliged the Soviet Government to tolerate the contamination of its citizens by some "alien" ideologies. Consequently, until his death early in March, 1953, Stalin gave much attention to an ideological purge which even invaded the hitherto immune field of natural science. Jews were signaled out for special reprobation as "cosmopolites" and admirers of the "rotten West."

The leading role of the Great Russians among the other peoples of the Soviet Union was forcefully emphasized. Soviet spokesmen show themselves eager to appear as an integral part of the Great Russian stream of history. On the occasion of the celebration of the Pushkin centennial Russia was declared to be a leading nation because she gave to the world Pushkin and Lenin.

Bolshevism Will Pass

Already the Soviet sphere of influence extends to eight hundred million human beings, thirty-two per cent of the globe's total. Among the enemies in the West, Soviet Russia has selected as the chief antagonist the tiny Vatican enclave. On the surface the odds appear hopeless. They would not have seemed so, however, to one of the world's supreme military geniuses. "There are only two powers in the world, the sword and the spirit," said Napoleon after his downfall. "In the long run, the sword is always defeated by the spirit."

The gray miasma of Bolshevism, a noxious effluvium that emanated from Western atheistic materialism, persisted on Russian soil only because it had absorbed in a perverted form ancient Russian ideals. But the misery of the Soviet period will one day pass, as did the darkness of the Tartar yoke centuries ago. Then, for the first time since Czar Basil II rejected union with the Western Church in 1441, Catholic apostles will not be prevented by despotic rulers from establishing contact with the Russian masses.

Under the guidance of the Holy See devoted Catholic priests have been preparing for the coming of this long-desired apostolate. Orthodox clergy would be attracted by their zeal, as they were by the sanctity of Exarch Leonidas Feodorov; Russian peasants would desire to become members of their religion, as they once wished for religious union with the great Metropolitan Shepticky; and the conversions won by the heroic Father Potapii Emilianov in southern Russia would be duplicated throughout the immense, vital land.

Then the dreams of Yury Krijanitch, of Peter Chaadaiev, and of Vladimir Soloviev would come true. A Russia reunited with the Holy See would realize her people's persistent messianic ideal of promoting the universal brotherhood of man. She would link East and West in the Universal Church, the Mystical Body of Christ. "Apart from God, Who is the very principle of Unity, no union is possible," wrote Vladimir Soloviev.[10]

Footnotes to Chapter Seventeen

[1] Camille M. Cianfarra, *The Vatican and the Kremlin,* pp. 49–52.
[2] N. S. Timasheff, *Religion in Soviet Russia,* pp. 49–79.
[3] Oscar Halecki, *Eugenio Pacelli,* pp. 129 f.
[4] Leopold Braun, *Worldmission,* December, 1950, "Catholics Behind the Iron Curtain," pp. 81 f.
[5] N. S. Timasheff, *op. cit.,* pp. 158–60.
[6] David J. Dallin, *The Real Soviet Russia,* pp. 67 f.

[7] Camille M. Cianfarra, *op. cit.*, pp. 62–87.
[8] Gary MacEoin, *The Communist War on Religion*, pp. 21–56; 75–169; 188–214.
[9] N. S. Timasheff, "Religion in Russia, 1941–1950," in *The Soviet Union*, a symposium edited by Waldemar Gurian, pp. 181, 266 f.
[10] Vladimir Soloviev, *Russia and the Universal Church*, pp. 9 f.

Selected Bibliography

General

ABRAHAM, G., *On Russian Music*. New York: Charles Scribner's Sons, 1939.

ALEXINSKY, Gregor, *Russia and Europe*. Translated by Bernard Miall. New York: Charles Scribner's Sons, 1917.

AMMANN, A. M., *Storia della Chiesa Russa*. Turin: Unione Tipografico, Editrice Torinese, 1948.

ARSENIEV, N., *Mysticism and the Eastern Church*. London, 1926.

BESTUSHEV-RIUMIN, K. N., *Geschichte Russlands*. Mittau, 1877.

BRIAN-CHANINOV, Nicolas, *L'Eglise Russe*. Paris: Chez Bernard Grasset, 1928.

BRÜCKNER, A., *Geschichte Russlands*. Two volumes. Gotha: F. A. Perthes, 1896.

BULGAKOV, S., *The Orthodox Church*. London: Centenary Press, 1938.

Cambridge Modern History. Cambridge: Cambridge University Press, 1934.

DANZAS, J. N., *The Russian Church*. Translated by Olga Bennigsen. New York: Sheed and Ward, 1936.

DULLES, Foster Rhea, *The Road to Teheran*. [The story of Russia and the United States, 1781–1943.] Princeton: Princeton University Press, 1944.

FEDOTOV, G. P., editor, *A Treasury of Russian Spirituality*. New York: Sheed and Ward, 1948.

FORTESCUE, Adrian, *The Orthodox Eastern Church.* London: Catholic Truth Society, 1920.

————, *The Uniate Eastern Churches.* [Excellent introductory chapter on Uniates in general.] New York: Benziger Brothers, 1923.

GORODETZKY, N., *The Humiliated Christ in Modern Russian Thought.* London, 1938.

GUERNEY, Bernard Guilbert, editor, *A Treasury of Russian Literature.* New York: The Vanguard Press, 1943.

GUTERMAN, N., translator, *Russian Fairy Tales.* New York: Pantheon, 1945.

HAMMER, J. de, *Histoire de l'Empire ottoman.* Eighteen volumes. Paris, 1835–1841.

HARPER, Samuel N., *The Russia I Believe In.* Chicago: University of Chicago Press, 1945.

HOETZSCH, Otto, *Russland.* Berlin: Georg Reimar, 1917.

HRUSZEWSKI, M., *Geschichte des Ukrainischen (Ruthenischen) Volkes.* Leipzig: Teubner, 1906.

ISWOLSKY, Helen, *Soul of Russia.* New York: Sheed and Ward, 1943.

KARAMSIN, M., *Histoire de l'Empire Russe.* Two volumes. Paris, 1918.

KERNER, Robert J., *Slavic Europe, a Bibliography.* Cambridge, Massachusetts: Harvard University Press, 1918.

KERNER, Robert J., *The Urge to the Sea: The Course of Russian History.* [The role of rivers, portages, forts, monasteries, and furs.] Berkeley and Los Angeles: University of California Press, 1942.

KONDAKOV, N. P., *The Russian Icon.* Oxford: Clarendon Press, 1927.

KORNILOV, Alexander, *Modern Russian History.* Revised edition. New York: Alfred A. Knopf, 1943.

KOSTOMAROV, N., *Russische Geschichte.* Leipzig, 1886.

KOVALEVSKY, Maxim, *Russian Political Institutions.* Chicago, 1902.

LEGRAS, J., *L'Âme Russe.* Paris: Flammarion, 1934.

LEROY-BEAULIEU, Anatole, *L'Empire des Tsars et les Russes.* Three volumes. Fourth edition. Paris, 1897–98.

LYASHCHENKO, Peter I., *History of the National Economy of Russia to the 1917 Revolution.* New York: The Macmillan Company, 1950.

MASARYK, T. G., *The Spirit of Russia.* [Studies in history, literature and philosophy.] Two volumes. Translated by Eden and Cedar Paul. London: Allen and Unwin, 1919.

MAVOR, J., *An Economic History of Russia.* London: J. M. Dent and Sons, Ltd., 1925.

MAYNARD, John, *Russia in Flux.* New York: The Macmillan Company, 1949.

MILIUKOV, Paul (with Seignobos and Eisenmann), *Histoire de Russie.* Two volumes. Paris, 1935.

———, *Outlines of Russian Culture.* Edited by M. Karpovich. Three volumes. Philadelphia: University of Pennsylvania Press, 1942.

MIRSKY, D. S., *A History of Russian Literature.* New York: Alfred A. Knopf, 1949.

———, *Russia: A Social History.* London: Cresset Press, 1930.

MOUSSET, Albert, *Histoire de Russie.* Paris: Société d'Editions Françaises et Internationales, 1945.

NAZAREVSKY, V. V., *Histoire de Moscou depuis les origines jusqu'à nos jours.* Paris, 1932.

NEWMARCH, Rosa, *The Russian Arts.* New York: E. P. Dutton and Company, 1916.

PARES, Bernard, *A History of Russia.* Fifth edition. New York: Alfred A. Knopf, 1948.

PLATONOV, S. F., *History of Russia.* Translated by E. Aronsberg. New York: The Macmillan Company, 1925.

ROUËT DE JOURNEL, M. J., *Monachisme et Monastères Russes,* Paris: Payot, 1952.

SEEGER, Elizabeth, *The Pageant of Russian History.* New York: Longmans, Green and Company, 1950.

SIMMONS, Ernest J., *An Outline of Modern Russian Literature (1880–1940).* Ithaca, N. Y.: Cornell University Press, 1943.

SLONIM, Marc, *The Epic of Russian Literature.* New York: Oxford University Press, 1950.

SPECTOR, Ivar, *An Introduction to Russian History and Culture.* New York: D. Van Nostrand Company, 1950.

STRAKHOVSKY, Leonid I., *A Handbook of Slavic Studies.* Cambridge, Mass.: Harvard University Press, 1949.

SUMNER, B. H., *A Short History of Russia.* New York: Reynal and Hitchcock, 1943.

TROITSKY, S. V., and MINNS, G. H., "Russian Church," *Hasting's Encyclopedia of Religion and Ethics.* Volume X, New York, 1919.

VERNADSKY, George, *A History of Russia.* New York: Home Library, 1944.

————, *Political and Diplomatic History of Russia.* Boston: Little, Brown and Company, 1936.

WALLACE, D. Mackenzie, *Russia.* New York: Henry Holt and Company, 1878.

WIENER, Leo, *Anthology of Russian Literature.* Two volumes. New York, 1902–03.

WILLIAMS, Henry Smith, *The Historians' History of the World.* Volume XVII. New York: The Encyclopaedia Britannica Company, 1904.

YARMOLINSKY, Avrahm, editor, *A Treasury of Great Russian Short Stories.* (Pushkin to Gorky.) New York: The Macmillan Company, 1946.

———, *A Treasury of Russian Verse.* New York: The Macmillan Company, 1949.

ZERNOV, N. M., *Moscow, The Third Rome.* [Religious situation in Russia prior to the Revolution.] London: Society for the Promotion of Christian Knowledge, 1937.

———, *The Russians and Their Church.* New York: The Macmillan Company, 1945.

Ancient and Kievan Russia

(Origins to year 1237)

Acta Sanctorum Bollandiana. Brussels, 1894 ff., in progress.

Ark, The. Catholic monthly published by the Ukrainian Catholic Diocese, Stamford, Connecticut.

BAUMGARTEN, N. de, *Aux origines de la Russie.* Rome, 1939.

———, *Saint Vladimir et la conversion de la Russie.* Rome, 1932.

BRÉHIER, Louis, *L'Eglise et L'Orient au Moyen Age: Les Croisades.* Second edition. Paris: Librairie Victor Lecoffre, 1907.

BUXTON, D. R., *Russian Medieval Architecture.* Cambridge: Cambridge University Press, 1934.

Cambridge Medieval History. Volume IV. New York: The Macmillan Company, 1927.

CHADWICK, N. K., *Russian Heroic Poetry.* Cambridge: Cambridge University Press, 1932.

CHAMBERLIN, William Henry, *The Russian Enigma.* New York: Charles Scribner's Sons, 1943.

Chronicle of Novgorod. Edition of Camden Society, London, 1914.

DVORNIK, F., *Les Slavs, Byzance et Rome au IXe siecle.* Paris: Champion, 1926.

ECK, Alexandre, *Le Moyen Age Russe.* Paris: Maison du Livre Etranger, 1933.

EUSEBIUS, *Church History.* Translated by A. S. McGiffert. New York, 1904.

EVANS, A. P., editor, *Medieval Russian Laws.* New York: Columbia University Press, 1947.

FEDOTOV, G. P., *The Russian Religious Mind: Kievan Christianity.* Cambridge, Massachusetts: Harvard University Press, 1946.

GOETZ, L. K., *Deutsch-russische Handelsgeschichte des Mittelalters.* Lübeck, 1922.

Holy Virgin's Descent into Hell, in Leo Wiener's *Anthology of Russian Literature.* Volume I, pp. 96–100.

Igor, Lay of the Host of, Bernard Guilbert Guerney, *A Treasury of Russian Literature,* pp. 5–33.

JAKOBSON, Roman, and SIMMONS, Ernest J., Editors, *Russian Epic Studies,* pp. 87–97. Philadelphia: American Folklore Society, 1949.

KONCEVICIUS, Joseph B., *Russia's Attitude Towards Union With Rome* (9th–16th centuries). Second edition. Washington, D. C., 1927.

LATOURETTE, Kenneth Scott, *A History of the Expansion of Christianity.* Volume II, New York: Harper and Brothers, 1938.

LEIB, B., *Rome, Kiev et Byzance à la fin du XIe siècle.* Paris: Picard, 1924.

MACLEAR, G. F., *Conversion of the West: The Slavs.* New York: Pott, Young, and Company, 1879.

MAGNUS, L. A., *The Heroic Ballads of Russia.* New York: E. P. Dutton and Company, 1921.

MANN, Horace K., *The Lives of the Popes in the Middle Ages.* Volumes VI, XII, XIII. St. Louis, Missouri: B. Herder Book Company, 1925.

NESTOR, *Chronicle,* in Leo Wiener's *Anthology of Russian Literature.* Volume I, pp. 65–71.

————, *Life of St. Theodosius,* in *A Treasury of Russian Spirituality,* edited by G. P. Fedotov, pp. 11–48.

NIEDERLE, L., *Manuel de l'antiquité slave.* Paris: Champion, 1927.

PALMIERI, A., *Le origini del canto liturgico russo.* Rassegna Gregoriana, VI. Rome, 1907.

PICHLER, A., *Geschichte der kirchlichen Trennung zwischen dem Orient und Okzident von den ersten Anfängen bis zur jüngsten Gegenwart.* Two volumes. Munich, 1864–65.

PIERLING, Paul, *La Russie et le Saint-Siège.* Etudes diplomatiques. Volume I. Second edition. Paris: Plon-Nourrit, 1906.

POTOCEK, Cyril J., *Saints Cyril and Methodius.* New York: P. J. Kenedy and Sons, 1941.

RAMBAUD, Alfred, *La Russie épique.* Paris, 1876.

RESSE, G., *Music in the Middle Ages.* New York: W. W. Norton and Company, 1940.

ROSTOVTSEV, M. I., *Les Origines de la Russie Kievienne.* Paris, 1922.

STANLEY, A. P., *Lectures on the History of the Eastern Church.* New York, 1884.

THOMSEN, V., *The Relation Between Ancient Russia and Scandinavia.* London, 1877.

VERDIÈRE, S. J., *Origines catholiques de l'Eglise russe.* Paris, 1856.

VERNADSKY, George, *Ancient Russia.* New Haven: Yale University Press, 1943.

———, *Kievan Russia* (878–1237). New Haven: Yale University Press, 1948.

VLADIMIR MONOMAKH, *His Instruction to His Children,* Leo Wiener's *Anthology of Russian Literature,* Volume I, pp. 50–56.

ZERNOV, N., *Saint Sergius, Builder of Russia.* New York: The Macmillan Company, 1939.

Muscovite Russia (1237–1689)

American Historical Review. Published by the American Historical Association, New York City, N. Y.

Ark, The. Catholic monthly published by the Ukrainian Catholic Diocese, Stamford, Connecticut.

ATTWATER, Donald, *The Catholic Eastern Churches.* Milwaukee: The Bruce Publishing Company, 1935.

AVRIL, P., *Voyage en divers Etats d'Europe et d'Asie pour découvrir un nouveau chemin à la Chine.* Paris, 1692.

AVVAKUM, Archpriest, *Autobiography.* Translated by Jane Harrison and Hope Mirrlees. London: Hogarth Press, 1926.

BARONIUS, Cesare, *Annales ecclesiastici.* Venice, 1739.

BEUCLER, André, *La Vie de Ivan le Terrible.* Paris: Librairie Gallimard, 1931.

BRÉHIER, Louis, *L'Eglise et l'Orient au Moyen Age: Les Croisades.* Paris: Librairie Victor Lecoffre, 1907.

Bury, J. B., "Russia (1462–1682)," *The Cambridge Modern History.* Volume V, pp. 477–517.

Buxton, D., *Russian Medieval Architecture.* New York: The Macmillan Company, 1934.

Cambridge Medieval History. Volume IV. New York: The Macmillan Company, 1927.

Chronicle of Novgorod. Edition of Camden Society, London, 1914.

Contarini, Ambrogio, *Journal.* Venice, 1487.

Eck, Alexandre, *Le Moyen Age Russe.* Paris: Maison du Livre Étranger, 1933.

Epiphanius the Wise, *The Life, Acts and Miracles of Our Revered and Holy Father Abbot Sergius,* in *A Treasury of Russian Spirituality,* edited by G. P. Fedotov, pp. 50–84.

Fisher, Raymond H., *The Russian Fur Trade,* 1550–1700. Berkeley and Los Angeles: University of California Press, 1943.

Fletcher, Giles, *On the Russe Commonwealth.* London, 1591.

Forstetter, Michel, *Voyageurs Etrangers en Russie* [10th–20th centuries]. Vevey, Switzerland: La Table Ronde, 1947.

Gagarin, Ivan, *The Russian Clergy.* Translated by Charles Du Gard Makepeace. London: Burns and Oates, 1872.

Geddie, John, *The Russian Empire.* London: T. Nelson and Sons, 1882.

Gerrare, Wirt, *The Story of Moscow.* London: J. M. Dent and Company, 1900.

Gogol, Nicolai V., *Taras Bulba.* [Describes the Cossacks' championship of the famous Orthodox Kievan Academy.] Translated by Isabel F. Hapgood. New York: Alfred A. Knopf, 1931.

GOYAU, Georges, in *For Joan of Arc,* by nine members of the French Academy. New York: The Macmillan Company, 1930.

GROUSSET, René, *The Civilizations of the East: India.* Translated by Catherine Alison Phillips. New York: Alfred A. Knopf, 1931.

GUÉPIN, A., *Un apôtre de l'Union des Églises au XVIIe siècle. Saint Josaphat.* Second edition. Paris, 1897.

HAKLUYT, Richard, *The principal Navigations, Voyages, Traffiques and Discoveries of the English Nation.* Volumes II and III. Glasgow, 1903.

HARNEY, Martin P., *The Jesuits in History.* New York: The America Press, 1941.

HEARD, A. F., *The Russian Church and Russian Dissent.* New York, 1887.

HERBERSTEIN, Sigismund von, *Rerum Moscovitarum commentarii.* Vienna, 1549.

IVAN THE TERRIBLE, *Letter to Prince Kurbski,* in Leo Wiener's *Anthology of Russian Literature.* Volume I, pp. 121–26.

KARAMZIN, N. M., *Geschichte Russlands.* Twelve volumes. Leipzig, 1820–1833.

KARTTUNEN, L., *Antonio Possevino, un diplomat pontifical au XVIe siècle.* Lausanne, 1908.

KLUCHEVSKY, V. O., *A History of Russia.* Translated by C. J. Hogarth. Five volumes. London, 1911–1927.

KONCEVICIUS, Joseph B., *Russia's Attitude Towards Union with Rome* (9th–16th centuries). Second edition. Washington, D. C., 1927.

KRIZHANICH, Yuri, *On Foreigners,* in Leo Wiener's *Anthology of Russian Literature.* Volume I, pp. 134–36.

KULSZYNSKI, J., *Specimen Ecclesiae Ruthenicae.* Rome, 1733.

Kurbski, Andrey Mikhaylovich, *Letter to Ivan the Terrible,* in Leo Wiener's *Anthology of Russian Literature.* Volume I, pp. 115–20.

Lamb, Harold, *The March of Muscovy* (1400–1648). Garden City, N. Y.: Doubleday and Company, Inc., 1948.

———, *The City and the Tsar* (1648–1762). Garden City, N. Y.: Doubleday and Company, Inc., 1948.

Latourette, Kenneth Scott, *A History of the Expansion of Christianity.* Volume II. New York: Harper and Brothers, Publishers, 1938.

Le Quien, M., *Oriens Christianus.* Three volumes. Paris, 1740.

Likowski, E., *Die ruthenisch—römische Kirchenvereinigung.* Freiburg, 1904.

Mann, Horace K., *The Lives of the Popes in the Middle Ages.* Volume XIV. St. Louis: B. Herder Book Co., 1928.

Mansi, J. D., *Sacrorum conciliorum collectio.* Thirty-one volumes. Florence and Venice, 1759–1798.

Margaret, Jacques, *Etat de l'Empire de Russie et Grand Duché de Moscovie.* Paris, 1607.

Massa, Isaac, *Histoires des guerres de la Moscovie* (1601–1610). Two volumes. Brussels, 1866.

Merimée, Prosper, *Demetrius the Imposter.* London: Bentley, 1853.

Nikitin, Athanassius, *Travel to India,* in Leo Wiener's *Anthology of Russian Literature.* Volume I, pp. 111–13.

Nilus Sorsky, St., *The Tradition to the Disciples,* in *A Treasury of Russian Spirituality,* edited by G. P. Fedotov, pp. 85–94.

Olearius, Adam, *The voyages and travels of the ambassadors from the duke of Holstein to the great Duke of Muscovy.* Translated by J. Davis. London: 1662.

PALMER, W., *The Patriarch Nikon.* Six volumes. London: Trubner, 1871–1876.

PASCAL, P., *Avvakum et les débuts du Raskol.* Paris: H. Champion, 1938.

PASTOR, Ludwig von, *The History of the Popes from the Close of the Middle Ages.* Thirty-four volumes. St. Louis: B. Herder Book Company, 1923–1941.

PELESZ, J., *Geschichte der Union der ruthenischen Kirche mit Rom, von den ältesten Zeiten bis auf die Gegenwart.* Vienna, 1878.

PICHLER, A., *Geschichte der kirchlichen Trennung zwischen dem Orient und Okzident von den ersten Anfängen bis zur jüngsten Gegenwart.* Two volumes. Munich, 1864–65.

PIERLING, Paul, *La Russie et le Saint-Siège.* Études diplomatiques. Volumes I, II, III, IV. Paris: Plon-Nourrit, 1897–1907.

———, "Le mariage d'un Tsar au Vatican," *Revue des Questions Historiques,* October, 1887, pp. 353–97. Paris, 1887.

———, *Papes et Tsars (1547–1597).* Paris, 1890.

———, *Rome et Démétrius d'après des documents nouveaux.* Paris, 1878.

PLATONOV, S. F., *Boris Godounov, Tsar de Russie (1598–1605).* Translated from the Russian by H. de Witte. Paris: Payot, 1929.

———, *La Russie moscovite.* Paris, 1932.

POSSEVINO, Antonio, *Moscovia et alia opera.* Vilna, 1587.

RAMBAUD, Alfred, *A Popular History of Russia.* Volumes I and II. Boston: Dana Estes and Charles E. Lauriat, 1882.

ROWBOTHAM, Arnold H., *Missionary and Mandarin.* Berkeley and Los Angeles: University of California Press, 1942.

RYLYEEV, Kondrati Feodorovich, *Ivan Susanin,* in Leo Wiener's *Anthology of Russian Literature.* Volume II, pp. 88–92.

SCOLARDI, Paulin-Gérard, *Krijanich.* Paris: Éditions A. et J. Picard et Compagnie, 1947.

SMURLO, E., *Le Saint-Siège et l'Orient orthodoxe russe.* (1609–1654.) Prague, 1928.

SOMMERVOGEL, Carlos, *Bibliothèque de la Compagnie de Jésus.* Paris, 1895. (For Possevino, see volume VI.)

Song of the Princess Kseniya Borisovna, in Leo Wiener's *Anthology of Russian Literature.* Volume I, pp. 132 ff.

THEINER, Augustinus, *Annales ecclesiastici.* Three volumes. Rome, 1856.

————, *Vetera Monumenta Poloniae et Lithuaniae.* Four volumes. Rome, 1860–1864.

TOLSTOY, Alexey Konstantinovich, *The Death of Ivan the Terrible,* in Leo Wiener's *Anthology of Russian Literature.* Volume II, pp. 255–57.

TOLSTOY, George, *England and Russia.* 1553–1593. St. Petersburg, 1875.

TURGENEV, A. J., *Historica Russiae Monumenta.* Two volumes. St. Petersburg, 1841.

VERNADSKY, George, *Bohdan, Hetman of Ukraine.* New Haven: Yale University Press, 1942.

————, "The Heresy of the Judaizers and Ivan III," *Speculum.* Volume VIII (1933).

WALISZEWSKI, K., *Ivan the Terrible.* Philadelphia: J. B. Lippincott Company, 1904.

Zadonshchina (The Exploits beyond the Don), in Leo Wiener's *Anthology of Russian Literature.* Volume I, pp. 106–11.

ZIEGLER, Th., *Die Union des Konzils von Florenz in der russischen Kirche.* Würzburg, 1938.

Peter I to Alexander I (1689–1801)

ANTHONY, Katharine, *Catherine the Great.* Garden City, N. Y.: Garden City Publishing Company, Inc., 1925.

BAIN, R. Nisbet, "Charles XII and the Great Northern War," *The Cambridge Modern History.* Volume V, pp. 584–615.

———, *The Daughter of Peter the Great.* London, 1902.

———, *The First Romanovs* (1613–1725). London, 1905.

———, *Peter III, Emperor of Russia.* London, 1902.

———, "Peter the Great and His Pupils (1689–1730)," *The Cambridge Modern History.* Volume V, pp. 518–57.

———, "Russia Under Anne and Elizabeth," *The Cambridge Modern History.* Volume VI, pp. 301–28.

BOIS, J., "L'Église catholique en Russie sous Catherine II," in the *Revue d'histoire ecclésiastique,* January–April, 1909. Louvain, 1909.

BRAUN, Leopold, "The Faith and the Peoples of Russia," in *Mission Studies,* September, 1950. Quarterly review published by the Mission Secretariat, Washington, D. C.

BRAUN, M., *Der Aufsteig Russlands vom Wikingerstaat zur europäischen Grossmacht.* Leipzig, 1940.

BRIAN-CHANINOV, Nicolas, *Catherine II, Impératrice de Russie.* Paris: Payot, 1932.

BRÜCKNER, A., *Die Europäisierung Russlands.* Gotha, 1888.

———, *Katherina die Zweite.* Berlin, 1883.

CATHERINE II, *Instructions,* in *Documents of Catherine the Great,* edited by W. F. Reddaway, p. 256.

CHAILLOT, J. L., *Pius VII et les Jésuites, d'après des documents inédits.* Rome, 1879.

CORSI, Edward C., *Poland: Land of the White Eagle.* New York: Wyndham Press, 1933.

DERZHAVIN, Gabriel Romanovich, *God, An Ode,* in *A Treasury of Russian Literature,* edited by Bernard Guilbert Guerney, pp. 45 ff.

DOLGORUKI, Princess Natalia Borisovna, *Memoirs,* in Leo Wiener's *Anthology of Russian Literature.* Volume I, pp. 233–41.

Encyclopedia, The Catholic. Sixteen volumes. New York: Universal Knowledge Foundation, 1907–1914.

FORSTETTER, Michel, *Voyageurs Etrangers en Russie* [10th–20th centuries]. Vevey, Switzerland: La Table Ronde, 1947.

GAGARIN, Ivan, *L'Empereur Paul et le Père Gruber.* Lyons, 1879.

————, *The Russian Clergy.* Translated by Charles Du Gard Makepeace. London: Burns and Oates, 1872.

GOLOVKIN, Feodor, *La Cour et le Règne de Paul 1er.* Paris, 1905.

GORDON, Patrick, *Diary.* Aberdeen, 1859.

HARNEY, Martin P., *The Jesuits in History.* New York: The America Press, 1947.

HAUTECOEUR, L., *L'Architecture classique à Saint-Pétersbourg à la fin du XVIIIe siècle.* Paris, 1912.

HEARD, J. A., *The Life and Times of Nathalia Borissovna, Princess Dolgorookov.* London, 1857.

HÖTZSCH, Otto, "Catherine II," *The Cambridge Modern History.* Volume VI, pp. 657–701.

KLUCHEVSKY, V. O., *A History of Russia.* Translated by C. J. Hogarth. Five volumes. London, 1911–1927.

KOBEKO, D., *Der Caesarewitsch Paul Petrowitsch.* Berlin, 1886.

LAMB, Harold, *The City and the Tsar* (1648–1782). Garden City, N. Y.: Doubleday and Company, Inc., 1948.

LESCOEUR, L., *L'Eglise catholique en Pologne sous le gouvernement russe* (1772–1875). Two volumes. Paris: Plon, 1876.

LOBANOV-ROSTOVSKY, A., "Russia and Germany," *The Russian Review,* Spring, 1943, pp. 31 ff.

LOMONOSOV, Mikhail Vasilevich, *Letters to I. I. Shuvalov on Devotion to Science,* in Leo Wiener's *Anthology of Russian Literature.* Volume I, pp. 241–46.

MARTEL, A., *Michel Lomonosov et la langue littéraire russe.* Paris, 1933.

MEREZHKOVSKI, Dmitri Sergyeevich, *Peter and Alexis,* in *A Treasury of Russian Literature,* edited by Bernard Guilbert Guerney, pp. 863–75.

MOLLOY, Fitzgerald, *The Russian Court in the Eighteenth Century.* Two volumes. New York: Charles Scribner's Sons, 1905.

NOVIKOV, Nikolay Ivanovich, Extracts from *All Kinds of Things,* the *Drone,* and the *Painter,* in Leo Wiener's *Anthology of Russian Literature.* Volume I, pp. 326–41.

PERRY, John, *The State of Russia under the Present Czar.* London, 1716.

PIERLING, Paul, *La Russie et le Saint-Siège.* Études diplomatiques. Volumes IV and V. Paris: Plon-Nourrit, 1907, 1912.

POROSHIN, S. A., *Diary.* [Tutor of Paul I.] St. Petersburg, 1844.

PUSHKIN, Alexander S., *The Captain's Daughter.* [A story of the *Pugachev* Rebellion.] Translated by Natalie Duddington. London: J. M. Dent and Sons, 1928.

RADISHCHEV, Alexander Nikolaevich, *Journey from St. Petersburg to Moscow,* in Leo Wiener's *Anthology of Russian Literature.* Volume I, pp. 361–70.

RAMBAUD, Alfred, *A Popular History of Russia.* Volume II. Boston: Dana Estes and Charles E. Lauriat, 1882.

RAPPOPORT, Angelo S., *The Curse of the Romanovs* (Paul I and Alexander I). New York: McClure, Phillips and Company, 1907.

REDDAWAY, W. F., *Documents of Catherine the Great.* Cambridge: Cambridge University Press, 1931.

ROUËT DE JOURNEL, M. J., *Un Collège de Jésuites à St. Pétersbourg.* Paris: Perrin, 1922.

SAINT-SIMON, Duc de, *Mémoires complets et authentiques.* Volume IX. Paris, 1872.

SCHIEMANN, Th., *Die Ermordung Pauls I.* Berlin, 1902.

SCHILDER, N. K., *Histoire anecdotique de Paul 1er.* Taken from the Russian by D. de Benckendorff. Paris, 1889.

SIMEON POLOTSKI, *On the Birth of Peter the Great,* in Leo Wiener's *Anthology of Russian Literature.* Volume I, pp. 149–51.

STUPPERICH, R., *Staatsgedanke und Religionspolitik Peters des Grossen.* Berlin, 1936.

SUVOROV, Alexander V., *Correspondenz des Fürsten Italiisky Grafen Suworoff-Rimniksky über die russische-österreichische Campagne im Jahr 1799.* Two volumes. Leipzig, 1835.

THEINER, Augustin, *Vicissitudes de l'Eglise catholique des deux rites en Pologne et en Russie.* Two volumes. Paris: Sagnier et Bray, 1843.

TYCHON OF ZADONSK, St., *Letters,* in *A Treasury of Russian Spirituality,* edited by G. P. Fedotov, pp. 225–39.

VOGUÉ, E. Melchior de, *Le fils de Pierre le Grand.* Paris, 1884.

————, *The True Story of Mazeppa.* London, 1884.

WALISZEWSKI K., *Pierre le Grand.* Third edition. Paris: Plon-Nourrit, 1897.

———, *L'héritage de Pierre le Grand.* Paris, 1900.

———, *The Romance of an Empress: Catherine II of Russia.* New York: D. Appleton and Company, 1894.

ZALENSKI, Stanislas, *Les Jésuites de la Russie Blanche.* Translated from the Polish by A. Vivier. Two volumes. Paris: Letouzey et Ané, Editeurs, 1886.

Alexander I to Russian Revolution (1801–1917)

ALDANOV, Mark, "Count Witte," *The Russian Review,* November, 1941, pp. 56–64.

ALEXANDER, Grand Duke of Russia, *Once a Grand Duke.* New York: Farrar and Rinehart, Inc., 1932.

ALEXANDRA, Empress Consort of Nicholas II, *Letters of the Tsaritsa to the Tsar, 1914–1916.* London, 1923.

ALEXINSKY, Gregor, *Russia and the Great War.* London, 1915.

ANET, Claude, "March Revolution, 1917," in *Voyageurs Etrangers en Russie,* edited by Michel Forstetter, pp. 213–19.

ANONYMOUS, *The Way of a Pilgrim,* in *A Treasury of Russian Spirituality,* edited by G. P. Fedotov, pp. 280–345.

Ark, The. Catholic monthly published by the Ukrainian Catholic Diocese, Stamford, Connecticut.

ASKENAZY, S., "Russia (1815–1831)," *The Cambridge Modern History.* Volume X, pp. 413–44.

ATTWATER, Donald, *The Catholic Eastern Churches.* Milwaukee: The Bruce Publishing Company, 1935.

BARING, Maurice, *The Mainsprings of Russia.* London: Thomas Nelson and Sons, 1914.

———, *The Puppet Show of Memory.* Boston: Little, and Company, 1922.

———, *A Year in Russia.* [An objective and informing picture of the important year 1905–06.] London: Methuen, 1908.

BARYATINSKY, Vladimir, *Le Mystère d'Alexandre 1er*. Paris: Payot, 1906.

BERDYAEV, Nicholas, *Dostoyevsky.* Translated by Donald Attwater. New York: Sheed and Ward, 1934.

———, "Russian Religious Psychology," in *Vital Realities.* New York: The Macmillan Company, 1932.

BERENGIER, Theophile, *Les Martyrs uniates en Pologne.* Paris: Palmé, 1868.

BIRKHAEUSER, J. A., *History of the Church.* Fifth edition. New York: Fr. Pustet and Company, 1896.

BOLSHAKOFF, Serge, *Russian Nonconformity.* [The story of "unofficial" religion in Russia]. Philadelphia: The Westminster Press, 1950.

BOTKIN, Gleb, *The Real Romanovs.* New York: Fleming H. Revell Company, 1931.

BOUDOU, Adrien, *Le Saint-Siège et la Russie* (1814–1847). Volume I. Paris: Librairie Plon, 1922.

———, *Le Saint-Siège et la Russie* (1848–1883). Volume II. Paris: Editions Spes, 1923.

BRAUN, Leopold, "The Faith and the Peoples of Russia," in *Mission Studies,* September, 1950. Quarterly review published by The Mission Secretariat, Washington, D. C.

BRESHKOVSKAIA, Katerina, *Hidden Springs of the Russian Revolution.* Stanford, California: Stanford University Press, 1931.

BRIAN-CHANINOV, Nicholas, *Alexandre Ier*. Paris: Bernard Grasset, 1934.

BUCHANAN, George, *My Mission to Russia and Other Diplomatic Memories.* Two volumes. London: Cassell, 1923.

Cambridge Modern History. New York: Encyclopaedia Britannica, Inc., 1934.

CHEKHOV, Anton Pavlovich, *The Three Sisters,* in *A Treasury of Russian Literature,* edited by Bernard Guilbert Guerney, pp. 802–62.

CONSALVI, *Mémoires du cardinal Consalvi.* Two volumes. Paris, 1864.

CORSI, Edward C., *Poland, Land of the White Eagle.* New York: Wyndham Press, 1933.

CURTISS, John Shelton, *Church and State in Russia* (1900–1917). New York: Columbia University Press, 1940.

CZARTORYSKY, Adam F., *Mémoires.* Paris, 1887.

DOHERTY, Catherine de Hueck, *My Russian Yesterdays.* Milwaukee: Bruce Publishing Company, 1951.

DOSTOEVSKY, Fyodor, *The Brothers Karamazov.* Translated by Constance Garnett. New York: The Modern Library, 1937.

Encyclopaedia Britannica. Eleventh edition. New York: The Macmillan Company, 1911.

Encyclopedia, The Catholic. Sixteen volumes. New York: Universal Knowledge Foundation, 1907–1914.

FEDOTOV, G. P., "The Religious Sources of Russian Populism," *The Russian Review,* April, 1942, pp. 27–39.

FLORINSKY, Michael T., *End of the Russian Empire.* New Haven: Yale University Press, 1931.

FORSTETTER, Michel, *Voyageurs Étrangers en Russie* [10th–20th centuries]. Vevey, Switzerland: La Table Ronde, 1947.

FREDERIKSEN, O. J., "Alexander I and His League to End Wars," *The Russian Review,* Autumn, 1943, pp. 10–22.

FULÖP-MILLER, René, *Leo XIII.* New York: Longmans, Green and Company, 1937.

———, *Rasputin, the Holy Devil.* London: Putnam, 1928.

GARGARIN, Ivan, *Tendances catholiques dans la société russe.* Paris: C. Douniol, 1860.

GERRARD, Thomas J., "Vladimir Soloviev—The Russian Newman," *The Catholic World,* June, 1917, pp. 321–36.

GOGOL, Nicholas Vassilievich, *The Inspector General,* in *A Treasury of Russian Literature,* edited by Bernard Guilbert Guerney, pp. 161–238.

GOLOVINE, Ivan, *La Russie sous Nicholas Ier.* Paris: Capelle, 1845.

GOLOVINE, N., *The Russian Army in the World War.* New Haven: Yale University Press, 1931.

GONCHAROV, Ivan Aleksandrovich, *Oblomov,* in Leo Wiener's *Anthology of Russian Literature.* Volume II, pp. 259–71.

GORKY, Maxim, *Twenty-six men and a Girl,* in *A Treasury of Great Russian Short Stories,* edited by Avrahm Yarmolinsky, pp. 973–87.

GRAHAM, Stephen, *Tsar of Freedom: The Life and Reign of Alexander II.* New Haven: Yale University Press, 1935.

———, *With the Russian Pilgrims to Jerusalem.* London, 1913.

GURKO, V. I., *Features and Figures of the Past* [Government and opinion in the reign of Nicholas II]. Stanford University, California: Stanford University Press, 1939.

GUROWSKI, A. de, *Russia As It Is.* [During reign of Nicholas I.] Third edition. New York: D. Appleton and Company, 1854.

HARE, Richard, *Pioneers of Russian Social Thought.* [Studies of non-Marxian formation in nineteenth-century Russia and of its partial revival in the Soviet Union.] New York: Oxford University Press, 1952.

HASSARD, John R. G., *A Life of Pope Pius IX*. New York: The Catholic Publication Society Company, 1878.

HERBIGNY, Michel d', *Vladimir Soloviev, a Russian Newman*. Translated by A. M. Buchanan. London: Washbourne, 1918.

HERZEN, Alexander I., *Le Monde Russe et la Révolution*. Paris, 1860.

———, *Slavophiles and Panslavism,* in Leo Wiener's *Anthology of Russian Literature*. Volume II, pp. 236–42.

ISWOLSKY, A. P., *The Memoirs of Alexander Iswolsky*. London, 1920.

ISWOLSKY, Hélène, *La Vie de Michel Bakunin*. Paris: Galimard, 1930.

JOHN OF CRONSTADT, *My Life in Christ,* in *A Treasury of Russian Spirituality,* edited by G. P. Fedotov, pp. 346–416.

KARAMZIN, Nikolay Mikhaylovich, *History of the Russian State,* in Leo Wiener's *Anthology of Russian Literature*. Volume II, pp. 37–40.

KERENSKY, Alexander F., *The Prelude to Bolshevism*. New York: Dodd, Mead, 1919.

KOVALEVSKI, M. M., *La Crise Russe*. Paris, 1906.

KRAVCHINSKY, S. M. (Stepniak, pseud.) *The Russian Peasantry*. [Their Agrarian Condition, Social Life and Religion.] New York: Harper and Brothers, 1888.

KROPOTKIN, Prince P. A., *Memoirs of a Revolutionist*. [Period of Alexander II.] Boston and New York, 1899.

KRYLOV, Ivan Andreevich, *Fables,* in Leo Wiener's *Anthology of Russian Literature*. Volume II, pp. 41–46.

KUPRIN, Alexander, *Gambrinus*. [Glimpses of the revolution of 1905.] In *A Treasury of Great Russian Short Stories,* edited by Avrahm Yarmolinsky, pp. 946–71.

LACROIX, Paul, *Histoire de la Vie et du Règne de Nicholas Ier, Empereur de Russie.* Paris: Amyot, 1869.

LAHARPE, Frederick C., *Mémoires.* [Tutor of Alexander I.] Bern, 1864.

LATOURETTE, Kenneth Scott, *A History of the Expansion of Christianity.* Volume IV. New York: Harper and Brothers Publishers, 1941.

LAVRIN, Janko, *Dostoevsky.* New York: The Macmillan Company, 1947.

LEMCKE, Peter Henry, *Life and Work of Prince Demetrius Augustine Gallitzine.* New York: Longmans, Green and Company, 1940.

LENIN, Vladimir I., *Collected Works.* New York: International Publishers, 1927 ff.

LERMONTOV, Michael Urievich, *Testament,* in *A Treasury of Russian Literature,* edited by Bernard Guilbert Guerney, pp. 110 ff.

LEROY-BEAULIEU, Anatole, *Un homme d'état russe* (Nicholas Miliutine). Paris, 1884.

LESCOEUR, L., *L'Eglise catholique en Pologne sous le gouvernement russe* (1772–1785). Two volumes. [Very prejudiced in favor of Poland.] Paris: Plon, 1876.

LOWE, Charles, *Alexander III of Russia.* New York: The Macmillan Company, 1895.

MACCAFFREY, James, *History of the Catholic Church in the Nineteenth Century* (1789–1908). Volume I. Second edition. St. Louis: B. Herder Book Company, 1910.

MCCULLAGH, Francis, *The Bolshevik Persecution of Christianity.* New York: E. P. Dutton and Company, 1924.

MCSORLEY, Joseph, *Outline History of the Church by Centuries,* Eighth revised edition. St. Louis: B. Herder Book Company, 1949.

MAISTRE, Joseph de, *Correspondance diplomatique* (1811–1817). Two volumes. Paris, 1860.

———, *Soirées de St. Pétersbourg*. Lyons, 1836.

MARIE, Grand Duchess of Russia, *Education of a Princess*. New York: The Viking Press, 1931.

MASARYK, Thomas G., *The Spirit of Russia*. New York: The Macmillan Company, 1919.

MAURICE, F. B., "The Russo-Japanese War," *The Cambridge Modern History*. Volume XII, pp. 576–601.

MAZADE, C. de, *Alexandre Ier et le Prince Czartorysky*. Paris, 1865.

MEREJKOVSKY, D., *Tolstoy As Man and Artist: With an Essay On Dostoyevsky*. New York: Putnam, 1902.

MOCHULSKY, C., *Vladimir Soloviev*. Paris: Y.M.C.A. Press, 1937.

MOTOVILOV, Nicholas, *A Conversation with St. Seraphim of Sarov,* in *A Treasury of Russian Spirituality,* edited by G. P. Fedotov, pp. 266–79.

NABOKOV, Vladimir, *Conclusive Evidence*. [The story of a distinguished liberal leader and his family under Nicholas II.] New York: Harper and Brothers, 1951.

NAZAROFF, A., *Tolstoy, the Inconstant Genius: A Biography*. New York: Stokes, 1930.

NICHOLAS MIKHAILOVITCH, Grand Duke of Russia, *L'Empereur Alexandre Ier, Essai d'Etude Historique*. Two volumes. St. Petersburg: Manufacture des Papiers de l'Etat, 1912.

O'REILLY, Bernard, *Life of Pius IX*. New York: P. F. Collier, 1877.

———, *Life of Leo XIII*. Philadelphia: John C. Winston Company, 1903.

OSTROVSKY, Alexander Nikolaevich, *The Storm,* in Leo Wiener's *Anthology of Russian Literature*. Volume II, pp. 369–78.

PALÉOLOGUE, Maurice, *La Russie des Tsars.* Three volumes. [World War I, as seen by French Ambassador in Petrograd.] Paris: Plon Nourrit, 1922.

PARES, Bernard, *The Fall of the Russian Monarchy.* London: Jonathan Cape Ltd., 1939.

PERRIS, G. H., *Russia in Revolution.* New York: Brentano's, 1905.

PFLEGER, Karl, *Wrestlers With Christ.* Translated by E. I. Watkins. [Contains Chapters on Dostoyevsky, Vladimir Soloviev, and Berdyaev.] New York: Sheed and Ward, 1936.

PIERLING, Paul, *La Russie et le Saint-Siège.* Etudes diplomatiques. Volume V. Paris: Librairie Plon, 1912.

POBEDONOSTEV, K. P., *Reflections of a Russian Statesman.* Translated by R. C. Long. London, 1898.

POLIAKOFF, Vladimir, *Tragic Bride.* [Last Czarina.] New York: Appleton, 1928.

PUSHKIN, Alexander Sergyeevich, *The Lay of Oleg the Wise,* in Leo Wiener's *Anthology of Russian Literature.* Volume II, pp. 139–42.

RADZIWILL, Catherine, *The Last Tzarina.* New York: Lincoln MacVeagh, The Dial Press, 1928.

RAMBAUD, Alfred, *A Popular History of Russia.* Volumes II and III. Boston: Dana Estes and Charles E. Lauriat, 1882.

RAPPAPORT, Angelo S., *The Curse of the Romanovs* (Paul I and Alexander I). New York: McClure, Phillips and Company, 1907.

RIO, Pedro del, *A Chilian's Journey Round the World.* Santiago, Chile, 1884.

RODZIANKO, M. V., *The Reign of Rasputin.* London: A. M. Philpot, 1927.

SAMSON-HIMMELSTIERNA, *Russia under Alexander III.* New York: The Macmillan Company, 1893.

SCHIEMANN, T., *Geschichte Russlands unter Kaiser Nikolaus I.* Three volumes. Berlin, 1904–13.

SÉGUR, Philippe de, *La Campagne de Russie.* Paris: Nelson, Éditeurs, 1910.

SHEA, John Gilmary, *The Life of Pope Pius IX.* New York: Thomas Kelly, 1877.

SHILDER, N. K., *Emperor Alexander I.* Four volumes. St. Petersburg, 1897–98.

SKARIATINA, Irna, *A World Can End.* New York: Jonathan Cape and Harrison Smith, 1931.

SMOLKA, Stanislas, *Les Ruthènes et les problèmes religieux du monde russien.* Berne: F. Wyss, 1917.

SMUCKER, Samuel M., *The Life and Reign of Nicholas the First, Emperor of Russia.* Philadelphia: G. G. Evans, 1858.

SOLOVIEV, Vladimir, *Russia and the Universal Church.* English translation. London: Geoffrey Bles, Ltd., 1948.

SPECTOR, Ivar, *The Golden Age of Russian Literature.* Los Angeles: The Scholastic Press, 1939.

SPIRIDON, Archimandrite, *Mes Missions en Sibérie, Souvenirs d'un Moine Orthodox Russe.* Introduction and translation by Pierre Pascal. [The author lived from 1875 to some time after 1906.] Paris: Editions du Cerf, 1950.

STRAKHOVSKY, L., *L'Empereur Nicholas Ier et l'esprit national russe.* Louvain: Librairie Universitaire, 1928.

STSCHEPKIN, Eugen, "Russia under Alexander I and the Invasion of 1812," *The Cambridge Modern History.* Volume IX, pp. 483–505.

TARASOV-RODIONOV, A., *February 1917.* New York: Covici, Friede, 1931.

TARLÉ, Eugene, *Napoleon's Invasion of Russia, 1812.* New York: Oxford University Press, 1942.

TATISTCHEFF, Serge, *Alexander Ier et Napoléon.* Paris, 1891.

TIMASHEFF, N. S., *Religion in Soviet Russia* (1917–1942). New York: Sheed and Ward, 1942.

TOLSTOY, Leo, *Anna Karenina.* Translated by Constance Garnett. New York: Grosset and Dunlap.

————, *Sevastopol in December, 1854,* in *A Treasury of Great Russian Short Stories,* edited by Avrahm Yarmolinsky, pp. 461–74.

————, *War and Peace.* Translated by Louise and Aylmer Maude, New York: Simon and Schuster, 1942.

TOUMANOVA, N., *Anton Chekhov: The Voice of Twilight Russia.* New York: Columbia University Press, 1937.

TURGENEV, Ivan Sergyeevich, *Fathers and Sons,* in *A Treasury of Russian Literature,* edited by Bernard Guilbert Guerney, p. 420.

————, *The Singers,* in *A Treasury of Great Russian Short Stories,* edited by Avrahm Yarmolinsky, pp. 90–106.

TURGENEV, N. I., *La Russie et les Russes.* Three volumes. [A Decembrist and historian of the movement.] Paris, 1847.

VANDAL, A., *Napoléon et Alexandre Ier.* Paris, 1891.

WALISZEWSKI, K., *Le règne d'Alexandre Ier.* Paris: Pion-Nourrit, 1924.

WALSH, Edmund A., *The Fall of the Russian Empire.* New York: Blue Ribbon Books, 1931.

WEBER, Nicholas A., *A General History of the Christian Era.* Volume II. Washington, D. C.: The Catholic Education Press, 1924.

WEBSTER, James, *Travels through Crimea.* London, 1830.

WILLIAMS, H. W., *Russia of the Russians.* New York: Scribner's Sons, 1914.

WISEMAN, Cardinal, *Recollections of the Last Four Popes.* Boston: Patrick Donahoe, 1858.

WITTE, Count S. I., *Mémoires du Comte Witte.* French Translation. Paris, 1921.

ZALENSKI, Stanislas, *Les Jésuites de la Russie Blanche.* Translated from the Polish by A. Vivier. Two volumes. Paris: Letouzey et Ané, Editeurs, 1886.

Russian Revolution to Present Time (1917–1953)

ANDERSON, Paul B., *People, Church and State in Modern Russia.* New York: The Macmillan Company, 1944.

BAERLEIN, H., *The March of the Seventy Thousand.* [The Czech Corps in Russia during the Civil War.] London: Leonard Parsons, 1926.

BASILY, N., *Russia Under Soviet Rule.* London: G. Allen and Unwin, 1938.

BEARDSLEY, Monroe C., "Berdyaev: Sibyl in Waste Land," *The Russian Review,* Spring, 1943.

BENNIGSEN, Georgii P., editor, *Religion in Russia.* [A collection of essays read at the Cambridge Summer school of Russian studies, 1939.] London: Burns, Oates and Washbourne, 1940.

BERDYAEV, Nicholas, *Freedom and the Spirit.* New York: Scribner and Sons, 1935.

————, *The Origin of Russian Communism.* Translated by G. French. London: G. Bles, 1937.

————, *Problème du Communisme.* Paris: Desclée de Brouwer, 1933.

————, "The Religion of Communism," in *Vital Realities.* New York: The Macmillan Company, 1932.

———, *The Russian Idea.* London: Geoffrey Bles, 1947.

BERG, L. S., *Natural Regions of the U.S.S.R.* Translated by Olga A. Tittelbaum. New York: The Macmillan Company, 1950.

BOLSHAKOFF, Serge, *The Christian Church and the Soviet State.* New York: The Macmillan Company, 1942.

———, *Russian Nonconformity.* [The story of "unofficial" religion in Russia.] Philadelphia: The Westminster Press, 1950.

BORNET, Francisque, *Je Revieus de Russie.* [Eye-witness account of heavy industry, the treatment of enemy aliens, and the survival of religion in the Soviet Union. The author, a French engineer, was in Russia from 1909 to 1946.] Paris: Librairie Plon, 1947.

BRAUN, Leopold, "Catholics Behind the Iron Curtain," in *Worldmission,* December, 1950. Quarterly review published by The Mission Secretariat, Washington, D. C.

———, "The Faith and the Peoples of Russia," in *Mission Studies* (renamed *Worldmission*), September, 1950.

BUKHARIN, N., *Historical Materialism.* New York: International Publishers, 1925.

BULLITT, William C., *The Great Globe Itself.* New York: Charles Scribner's Sons, 1946.

CARR, Edward H., *The Bolshevik Revolution* (1917–1923). New York: The Macmillan Company, 1951.

———, *Karl Marx.* London: J. M. Dent and Sons, 1934.

CHAMBERLIN, William Henry, *The Russian Enigma.* New York: Charles Scribner's Sons, 1943.

———, *The Russian Revolution.* (1917–1921.) Two volumes. New York: The Macmillan Company, 1935.

———, *Russia's Iron Age.* Boston: Little, Brown and Company, 1935.

———, *Soviet Russia.* Boston: Little, Brown and Company, 1930.

CHURCHILL, Winston S., *The Hinge of Fate.* Boston: Houghton Mifflin Company, 1950.

———, *The World Crisis: The Aftermath.* [Allied intervention in Russia.] London: Thornton Butterworth, 1929.

CIANFARRA, Camille M., *The Vatican and the Kremlin.* New York: E. P. Dutton and Company, Inc., 1950.

CRANKSHAW, Edward, *Cracks in the Kremlin Wall.* New York: The Viking Press, 1951.

CURIE, Eve, *Journey Among Warriors.* Garden City, New York: Doubleday, Doran and Co., Inc., 1943.

DALLIN, David J., *Soviet Russia's Foreign Policy* (1939–1942). New Haven: Yale University Press, 1942.

———, *The New Soviet Empire.* New Haven: Yale University Press, 1951.

———, *The Real Soviet Russia.* New Haven: Yale University Press, 1944.

DERRICK, M., *Eastern Catholics Under Soviet Rule.* London: Sword of the Spirit, 1946.

DEUTSCHER, Isaac, *Stalin: A Political Biography.* New York: Oxford University Press, 1949.

DOYLE, Charles Hugo, *The Life of Pope Pius XII.* New York: Didier, 1945.

DUKES, Paul, *Red Dusk and the Morrow.* [Firsthand description of early Red Army by Englishman engaged in espionage work.] New York: Doubleday, Page, 1922.

DUSHNYCK, Walter, "Kremlin's Meretricious Use of the Orthodox Church," in *The Ark,* December, 1951, pp. 163 f., 172.

EASTMAN, Max, *Artists in Uniform: A Study of Literature and Bureaucratism.* New York: Alfred A. Knopf, 1934.

FEDOTOV, G. P., *The Russian Church since the Revolution.* New York: The Macmillan Company, 1928.

FISCHER, Louis, *The Soviets in World Affairs* (1917–1918). First published in 1930. Princeton: Princeton University Press, 1951.

FONTENELLE, R., *His Holiness Pope Pius XI.* Translated by M. E. Fowler, Cleveland, Ohio: The Sherwood Press, 1939.

FÜLÖP-MILLER, René, *The Mind and Face of Bolshevism.* New York: Putnam, 1928.

GOLDER, Frank A., editor, *Documents of Russian History, 1914–1917.* New York: The Century Company, 1927.

GOUZENKO, Igor, *This Was My Choice.* Toronto: J. M. Dent and Sons Limited, 1948.

GURIAN, Waldemar, *Bolshevism: Theory and Practice.* Translated by E. I. Watkin. New York: Sheed and Ward, 1935.

GURIAN, Waldemar, editor, *The Soviet Union* (A symposium). Notre Dame, Indiana: University of Notre Dame Press, 1951.

HALECKI, Oscar, *Eugenio Pacelli: Pope of Peace.* New York: Creative Age Press, Inc., 1951.

HALLE, Fannini W., *Women in Soviet Russia.* New York: Viking Press, 1935.

HARPER, Samuel N., *Civic Training in Russia.* Chicago: Chicago University Press, 1929.

HAUSER, Ernest O., "What Stalin Has in Mind for Catholics," *Saturday Evening Post,* September 22, 1951, pp. 19–21; 24–26.

HECKER, Julius F., *Religion and Communism.* [A study of religion and atheism in Soviet Russia.] London: Chapman and Hall, 1933.

HINDUS, Maurice, *Mother Russia* [Russians during World War II]. New York: Doubleday, Doran and Company, 1943.

———, *Red Bread* [Picture of peasants under collectivization.] New York: Harrison Smith, 1931.

HOLLIS, Christopher, *Lenin.* Milwaukee: Bruce Publishing Company, 1938.

ISWOLSKY, Helen, *Soviet Man Now.* London: Sheed and Ward, 1937.

JORRÉ, Georges, *L'U.R.S.S: La Terre et Les Hommes.* Paris: Société d'Editions Françaises et Internationales, 1946.

KARLGREN, Anton, *Bolshevist Russia.* [Excellent picture of Russian Peasantry, 1921–27.] London: G. Allen and Unwin, 1927.

KASENKINA, Oksana, *Leap To Freedom.* Philadelphia: J. B. Lippincott Company, 1949.

KAUN, A., *Maxim Gorky and His Russia.* New York: R. O. Ballou, 1931.

KERENSKY, Alexander F., *The Catastrophe.* New York: Appleton Century, 1927.

KOUDREY, Vladimir, *Once a Commissar.* New Haven: Yale University Press, 1937.

KRAVCHENKO, Victor, *I Chose Freedom.* Garden City, New York: Garden City Publishing Co., Inc., 1947.

———, *I Chose Justice.* New York: Charles Scribner's Sons, 1950.

KRIVITSKY, Walter G., *Stalin's Secret Service.* New York: Harper and Brothers, 1939.

LENIN, Vladimir I., *Collected Works.* New York: International Publishers, 1927–1932.

LEVINE, Isaac Don, *Stalin.* New York: Blue Ribbon Books, 1931.

Life Magazine, *Special U.S.S.R. Issue,* March 29, 1943.

LOCKHART, R. H. Bruce, *British Agent,* New York: G. P. Putnam's Sons, 1933.

LONDON, K., *The Seven Soviet Arts.* New Haven: Yale University Press, 1938.

LORIMER, F., *The Population of the Soviet Union: History and Prospects.* Geneva: League of Nations, 1946.

LOSSKY, N., "The Successors of Vladimir Soloview," *The Slavonic Review.* Volume III (1924).

LYONS, Eugene, *Assignment in Utopia.* New York: Harcourt, Brace and Company, 1937.

————, *Stalin, Czar of All the Russias.* Philadelphia: J. B. Lippincott Company, 1940.

MCCULLAGH, Francis, *The Bolshevik Persecution of Christianity.* New York: E. P. Dutton and Company, 1924.

MACEOIN, Gary, *The Communist War on Religion.* New York: The Devin-Adair Company, 1951.

MARIE, Grand Duchess of Russia, *Education of a Princess.* New York: The Viking Press, 1931.

MARTOV, J., and Dan, F., *Geschichte der Russischen Sozialdemokratie.* Berlin: J. H. W. Dietz Nachfolger, 1926.

MELGOUNOV, Sergey P., *The Red Terror of Russia.* London: J. M. Dent and Sons, 1926.

MIKHAILOV, Nicholas, *Land of the Soviets: A Handbook.* New York: Lee Furman, Inc., 1939.

MIKOLAJCZYK, Stanislaw, *The Rape of Poland.* New York: Whittlesey House, 1948.

MILIUKOV, Paul, *Russlands Zusammenbruch.* Two volumes. Berlin: Obelisk Verlag, 1926.

MIROV, N. T., *Geography of Russia.* New York: John Wiley and Sons, 1951.

MIRSKY, D. S., *Lenin.* Boston: Little, Brown and Company, 1931.

MOORAD, George, *Behind the Iron Curtain.* Philadelphia: Fireside Press, Inc., 1946.

MOUSSET, Albert, *Le Monde Slave.* Second Edition. Paris: Société d'Éditions Françaises et Internationales, 1946.

NAZAROFF, Alexander, *The Land of the Russian People.* New York: Lippincott, 1944.

PARES, Bernard, *The Fall of the Russian Monarchy.* London: Jonathan Cape Ltd., 1939.

———, *Russia.* New York: Penguin Books, 1945.

PETROV, Vladimir, *Soviet Gold: My Life as a Slave Laborer in the Siberian Mines.* New York: Farrar, Straus and Company, 1949.

POLIAKOV, Alexander, *Russians Don't Surrender.* Translated by Norbert Guterman. New York: E. P. Dutton and Company, 1943.

REED, John, *Ten Days That Shook the World.* New York: International Publishers, 1926.

ROPE, Henry E. G., *Benedict XV.* London: The Catholic Book Club, 1940.

ROSENBERG, Arthur, *A History of Bolshevism.* New York: Oxford University Press, 1934.

RÜHLE, Otto, *Karl Marx: His Life and Work.* Translated by Eden and Cedar Paul. New York: The New Home Library, 1943.

SAVINKOV, Boris, *Memoirs of a Terrorist.* New York: Albert and Charles Boni, 1931.

SCHUBART, Walter, *Russia and Western Man.* Translated by Amethé von Zeppelin. New York: Frederick Ungar Publishing Company, 1950.

SCHWARTZ, M. Alexander, *The Voice of Russia.* New York: E. P. Dutton and Company, 1921.

SCOTT, John, *Beyond the Urals.* [Life and work at Magnitogorsk.] Boston: Houghton Mifflin, 1942.

SERGE, Victor, *The Case of Comrade Tulayev.* Translated from the French by Willard R. Trask. New York: Doubleday and Company, 1950.

SHABAD, Theodore, *Geography of the USSR.* New York: Columbia University Press, 1951.

SHEEN, Fulton J., *Communism and the Conscience of the West.* Indianapolis-New York: The Bobbs-Merrill Company, 1948.

SIMONOV, Konstantine, *Days and Nights* (Siege of Stalingrad). Translated by Joseph Barnes. New York: Simon and Schuster, 1945.

SKOMOROVSKY, Boris, and MORRIS, E. G., *The Siege of Leningrad.* New York: E. P. Dutton and Company, 1944.

SLOSSER, G. I., *Christian Unity, Its History and Challenge.* London, 1929.

SMITH, Walter Bedell, *My Three Years in Moscow.* Philadelphia: J. B. Lippincott Company, 1950.

SOUVARINE, Boris, *Stalin, A Critical Survey of Bolshevism.* Translated by C. L. R. James. New York: Longmans, Green and Company, 1939.

SPINKA, Matthew, *The Church and the Russian Revolution.* New York: The Macmillan Company, 1927.

STALIN, Joseph V., *Leninism.* New York: International Publishers, 1928.

————, *The War of National Liberation.* New York: International Publishers, 1942.

STEINBECK, John, *A Russian Journal.* New York: The Viking Press, 1948.

STETTINIUS, Edward R., *Roosevelt and the Russians.* New York: Doubleday and Company, 1949.

STEVENS, Edmund, *This Is Russia—Uncensored.* New York: Didier, 1950.

STRUVE, Gleb, *Soviet Russian Literature.* London: G. Routledge and Sons, 1935.

TIMASHEFF, N. S., *Religion in Soviet Russia* (1917–1942). New York: Sheed and Ward, 1942.

————, "Russian Nationalism Under the Soviets," in *Thought,* September, 1945. New York: Fordham University quarterly.

————, *The Great Retreat.* [The Growth and Decline of Communism in Russia.] New York: E. P. Dutton and Company, Inc., 1946.

TROTZKY, Leon, *The History of the Russian Revolution.* Three volumes. New York: Simon and Shuster, 1932.

————, *Lenin,* New York: Minton, Balch and Company, 1925

VERNADSKY, George, *Lenin: Red Dictator.* New Haven: Yale University Press, 1931.

VULLIAMY, C., editor, *The Red Archives.* Translated by A. L. Hynes, London: Geoffrey Bles, 1929.

WALSH, Edmund A., *The Fall of the Russian Empire.* New York: Blue Ribbon Books, 1931.

————, *The Last Stand.* [First Five-Year Plan.] Boston: Little, Brown and Company, 1931.

————, *Total Empire: The Roots and Progress of World Communism.* Milwaukee: The Bruce Publishing Company, 1951.

WHITE, D. Fedotoff, *The Growth of the Red Army.* Princeton: Princeton University Press, 1944.

WILLIAMS, Albert Rhys, *The Russians, the Land, the People, and Why They Fight.* New York: Harcourt, Brace and Company, 1943.

WUYTS, A., *Le Patriarcat russe au Concile de Moscou de 1917–18.* Rome, 1947.

YAROSLAVSKY, E., *Religion in the U.S.S.R.* New York: International Publishers, 1934.

YELCHANINOV, Alexander, *Fragments of a Diary,* in *A Treasury of Russian Spirituality,* edited by G. P. Fedotov, pp. 417–85.

ZINOVIEV, Gregory, *Geschichte der Kommunistischen Partei Russlands.* Hamburg: Verlag Carl Hoym Nachfolger, 1923.

Readers familiar with the Russian language will find in *Storia della Chiesa Russa,* by A. M. Ammann, comprehensive lists of books in Russian which deal with the relations of Russia and the Western Church.

Index

A NOTE ON THE TYPE IN WHICH THIS BOOK IS SET

This book is set in Baskerville, an Intertype face, created from the original types used by John Baskerville, the eighteenth-century typefounder and printer. This type has long been considered one of the finest book types ever developed. The letters are wide and open and have a businesslike approach. The finer hairlines give exquisite delicacy. The heavier strokes give color and strength. The relation of the two in combination gives a brilliant effect and makes for easy reading. The book was composed and printed by the York Composition Company, Inc., of York, Pa., and bound by Moore and Company of Baltimore. The typography and design are by Howard N. King.